Mice & Rats - shrews, mole, voles, muskrat — pg. 35

Nutria, Beaver & Capybara — pg. 115

Bats — pg. 127

Squirrels & Gophers - chipmunk — pg. 133

Monkeys — pg. 157

Rabbits & Hare — pg. 165

Weasels & Skunks - mink, otter — pg. 177

Raccoons - coati — pg. 197

Armadillo & Opossum — pg. 205

Dogs - foxes, coyote, wolf — pg. 213

Cats - jaguarundi, bobcat, panther — pg. 229

Deer — pg. 241

Hog — pg. 253

Bear — pg. 257

Bison

Marine - dolphins, manatee

T0125464

Mammals
of **Florida**
—————————————*Field Guide*

by Stan Tekiela

Adventure Publications, Inc.
Cambridge, Minnesota

To naturalists everywhere who have committed to spreading the word of conservation.

ACKNOWLEDGMENTS

A heartfelt thanks to Rick and Nora Bowers, who greatly helped me obtain many of the photos for this book. Special thanks to the National Wildlife Refuge System and the many public and private state and local agencies for stewarding the lands that are critical to the wild mammals we love so much.

Edited by Sandy Livoti

Cover and book design by Jonathan Norberg

Silhouettes, tracks and range maps by Anthony Hertzel

Cover photo: Red Fox by Stan Tekiela
See pages 299-300 for photo credits by photographer and page number.

Copyright 2010 by Stan Tekiela
Published by Adventure Publications, Inc.
820 Cleveland St. S
Cambridge, MN 55008
1-800-678-7006
www.adventurepublications.net
ISBN-13: 978-1-59193-251-2
ISBN-10: 1-59193-251-3

TABLE OF CONTENTS

Introduction

Florida's Mammals 8

What Is a Mammal? 8

Identification Step-by-Step 10

Taxonomy of Florida's Mammals 12

Caution 12

Quick-Compare Pages 14

Sample Pages 31

The Mammals

Mice & Rats

Shrews 35

Moles 47

Mice 55

Rats 79

Voles 103

Muskrat 111

Nutria 115

Beaver 119

Capybara 123

Bats 127

Squirrels

Chipmunk 133

Flying Squirrel 137

Tree Squirrels 141

Pocket Gopher 153

Monkeys 157

Rabbits & Hare

Rabbits 165

Jackrabbit 173

Weasels

Weasel 177

Mink 181

Otter 185

Skunks 189

Raccoons

Raccoon 197

Coati 201

Armadillo 205

Opossum 209

Dogs

Foxes 213

Coyote 221

Wolf 225

Cats

Jaguarundi 229

Bobcat 233

Panther 237

Deer 241

Hog 253

Bear 257

Cattle

Bison 261

Marine

Dolphins 265

Manatee. 277

Glossary 280

Helpful Resources 285

Appendix: Taxonomy of Florida's Mammals 286

Check List/Index 296

Photo Credits 299

About the Author 301

FLORIDA'S MAMMALS

Florida is a great place for wildlife watchers! This state is one of the few places to see magnificent mammals, such as the elusive Florida Panther, along with many interesting animals such as the Nine-banded Armadillo. While West Indian Manatees swim in the rivers of Florida, Bobcats thrive in nearly all habitats across the state. No matter where you may be in Florida, there is a wide variety of mammals to see and enjoy.

Mammals of Florida Field Guide is an easy-to-use field guide to help the curious nature lover identify all species of mammals found in Florida. It is an all-photographic guide just for Florida, featuring full-color images of animals in their habitats. It is one in a series of unique field guides for Florida that includes birds, mammals and wildflowers.

WHAT IS A MAMMAL?

The first mammals appeared in the late Triassic Period, about 200 million years ago. These ancient mammals were small, lacked diversity and looked nothing like our current-day mammals. During the following Jurassic Period, mammal size and diversity started to increase. Mammals generally started to appear more like today's mammals in the Cenozoic Era, which occurred after the mass extinction of dinosaurs, about 60 million years ago.

Today, modern mammals are a large group of animals that includes nearly 5,500 species around the world, with more than 400 species in North America. Here in Florida we have 77 species, most native to the state. They range from the Least Shrew, a tiny mammal no larger than a human thumb, to the very large and majestic American Bison, which can grow to a length of 12 feet (3.7 m) and weigh up to 2,000 pounds (900 kg). Florida also has non-native (exotic) animals such as the Rhesus Monkey and Sambar Deer.

All mammals have some common traits or characteristics. Mammals have a backbone (vertebra) and are warm-blooded (endothermic). In endothermic animals, the process of eating and breaking down food in the digestive tract produces heat, which keeps the animal warm even on cold winter nights. Except during periods of hibernation or torpor, the body temperature of mammals stays within a narrow range, just as it does in people. Body temperature is controlled with rapid, open-mouthed breathing known as panting, by shunting blood flow to or away from areas with networks of blood vessels, such as ears, for cooling or conserving heat. When blood flows through vessels that are close to the surface of skin, heat is released and the body cools. When blood flows away from the surface of skin, heat is conserved.

Most mammals are covered with a thick coat of fur or hair. Fur is critical for survival and needs to be kept clean and in good condition. In some animals, such as the Northern River Otter, the fur is so thick it keeps the underlying skin warm and dry even while swimming. Just as birds must preen their feathers to maintain good health, animals spend hours each day licking and "combing" or grooming their fur. You can easily observe this grooming behavior in your pet cat or dog.

Mammals share several other characteristics. All females bear live young and suckle their babies with milk produced from the mammary glands. Mother's milk provides young mammals with total nourishment during the first part of their lives. Also, mammals have sound-conducting bones in their middle ears. These bones give animals the ability to hear as people do and, in many cases, hear much better.

Mammals are diphyodont, meaning they have two sets of teeth. There are milk or deciduous teeth, which fall out, and permanent teeth, also known as adult teeth. Adult teeth usually consist of incisors, canines, premolars and molars, but these categories can be highly variable in each mammal family. Teeth are often used to classify or group mammals into families in the same manner as the bill of a bird is used to classify or group birds into families.

Reproduction in mammals can be complex and difficult to understand. Many mammals have delayed implantation, which means after the egg and sperm have joined (impregnation), the resulting embryo remains in a suspended state until becoming implanted in the uterine wall. The delay time can be anywhere from a few days to weeks or months. An animal that becomes stressed from lack of food will pass the embryo out of the reproductive tract, and no pregnancy occurs. Conversely, well-fed mothers may have twins or even triplets. Bats and some other species store sperm in the reproductive tract over winter. Impregnation is delayed until spring, and implantation occurs right after impregnation. This process is known as delayed impregnation.

Most mammals are nocturnal, secretive and don't make a lot of noise, so they tend to go unnoticed. Signs of mammals, such as tracks or scat, are often more commonly seen than the actual animal. However, if you spend some time in the right habitat at the right time of day, your chances of seeing mammals will increase.

IDENTIFICATION STEP-BY-STEP

Fortunately, most large mammals are easy to identify and are not confused with other species. This is not the case, however, with small mammals such as mice or voles. Small animals, while plentiful, can be a challenge to correctly identify because they often have only minor differences in teeth or internal organs and bones.

This field guide is organized by families, starting with small animals, such as shrews and mice, and ending with large mammals such as bison and dolphins. Within each family section, the animals are in size order from small to large.

Each mammal has four to six pages of color photos and text, with a silhouette of the animal illustrated on the first description page. Each silhouette is located in a quick-compare tab in the upper right corner. Decide which animal group you are seeing, use the quick-compare tabs to locate the pages for that group, then compare the photos with your animal. If you aren't sure of the identity, the text on description pages explains identifying features that may or may not be easily seen. The first description page for each species also has a compare section with notes about similar species in this field guide. Other pertinent details and the naturalist facts in Stan's Notes will help you correctly identify your mammal in question. Photos of other species will help you identify all of the mammals of Florida.

Thus, every effort has been made to provide relevant identification information including range maps, which can help you eliminate some choices. Colored areas of the maps show where a species can be seen, but not the density of the species. While ranges are accurately depicted, they change on an ongoing basis due to a variety of factors. Please use the maps as intended–as a general guide only.

Finally, if you already know the name of your animal, simply use the index to quickly find the page and learn more about the species from the text and photos.

For many people, an animal's track or silhouette is all they might see of an animal. However, tracks in mud or sand and silhouettes are frequently difficult to identify. Special quick-compare pages, beginning on page 14, are a great place to start the identification process. These pages group similar kinds of animals and tracks side by side for easy comparison. For example, all hoofed animals, such as deer, are grouped in one section and all dog-like animals are grouped in another. Within the groupings, silhouettes and tracks are illustrated in relative size from small to large. This format allows you to compare one silhouette or track shape and size with another that is similarly shaped and sized. When you don't know whether you're seeing the silhouette or track of a coyote or wolf, a deer or other similar species, use the quick-compare pages for quick and easy reference.

To begin, find the group that your unknown silhouette or track looks similar to and start comparing. Since each group has relatively few animals, it won't take long to narrow your choices. A ruler can be handy to measure your track and compare it with the size given in the book. To confirm the identity of the silhouette or track and for more detailed information about the animal, refer to the description pages for the number of toes, length of stride and other distinguishing characteristics.

TAXONOMY OF FLORIDA'S MAMMALS

Biologists classify mammals based on their ancestry and physical characteristics. Florida mammals are grouped into 11 scientific orders. Charts with the scientific classification (taxonomy) are shown on the Appendix, pages 286-295. Each of the 11 charts starts with one of the orders and shows all scientific families and mammals in that particular order.

CAUTION

Hunting, trapping, possessing and other activities involving animals are regulated by the Florida Fish and Wildlife Conservation Commission. You should familiarize yourself with the laws and seasons before doing any kill trapping, live trapping and hunting.

As interesting as all of these animals are, resist any temptation to capture any animal for a pet. Wild animals, even babies, never make good pets. Wild animals often have specific dietary and habitat requirements that rarely can be duplicated in a captive situation, and many will not survive. In many cases, capturing animals for pets is also illegal. This practice not only diminishes the population, it reduces the possibility for future reproduction. Furthermore, some animals are uncommon in Florida, and their populations can be even more quickly depleted.

Live trapping of animals in an attempt to rid your yard of them rarely works. The removal of an animal from its habitat creates a void that is quickly filled with a neighboring animal or its offspring, recreating the original situation. Moreover, an unfortunate animal that is live trapped and moved to a new location often cannot find a habitat with an adequate food supply, shelter or a territory that is not already occupied. Animals that have been moved often die from exposure to weather, are struck by vehicles while crossing roads or killed by resident animals. With habitat ranges growing smaller every year, removing just one animal can have a direct impact on the local population of a species. We can all learn to live with our wild animals with just a few modifications to our yards and attitudes. Observe and record animals with your camera, but leave them where they belong–in the wild.

Encounters with wildlife often involve injured or orphaned animals. Many well-intentioned people with little or no resources or knowledge of what is needed try to care for such animals. Injured or orphaned animals deserve the best care, so please do the right thing if you find one and turn it over to a licensed professional wildlife rehabilitator. Information about wildlife rehabilitation in Florida is listed in the resource section of this field guide. The rehabilitation staff may often be able to give you updates on the condition of an animal you bring in and even when it is released. When you take an animal to a rehab center, you might also want to consider making a monetary donation to help cover the costs involved for its care.

Enjoy the Wild Mammals!

Stan

Body length measurements do not include tail.

Average size of the smallest and largest of this group compared to an 8" hand.

Silhouettes are in proportion by average body length. Tracks are in proportion by average largest foot. Front track is on the left and hind is on the right.

1⅞"

Least Shrew
pg. 35

⅛"   ⅜"

2½"
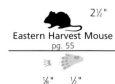
Eastern Harvest Mouse
pg. 55

⅛"   ½"

3½"

Southern Short-tailed Shrew pg. 43

⅜"   ½"

3¾"
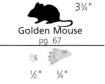
Golden Mouse
pg. 67

½"   ¾"

4⅞"
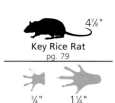
Key Rice Rat
pg. 79

¾"   1¼"

5"

Marsh Rice Rat
pg. 83

½"   1"

5"
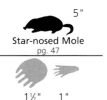
Star-nosed Mole
pg. 47

1½"   1"

8"

Round-tailed Muskrat
pg. 111

1"   1¾"

8⅛"

Florida Mouse
pg. 75

¾"   1"

9"
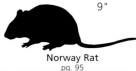
Norway Rat
pg. 95

1"   1½"

2½"

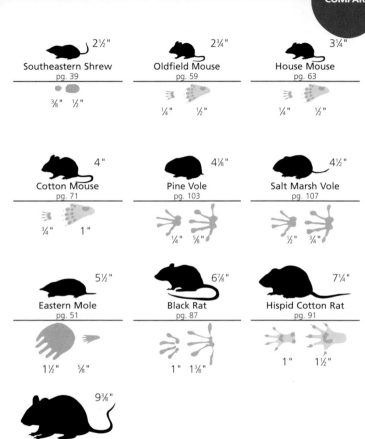

Southeastern Shrew
pg. 39

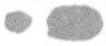
⅜" ½"

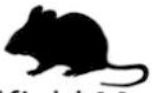
2¾"

Oldfield Mouse
pg. 59

¼" ½"

3¼"

House Mouse
pg. 63

¼" ½"

4"

Cotton Mouse
pg. 71

¾" 1"

4⅛"

Pine Vole
pg. 103

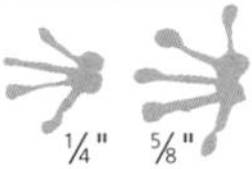
¼" ⅝"

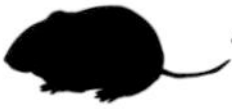
4½"

Salt Marsh Vole
pg. 107

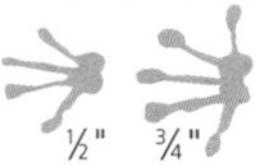
½" ¾"

5½"

Eastern Mole
pg. 51

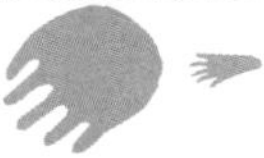
1½" ⅝"

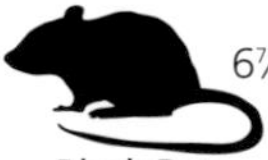
6⅞"

Black Rat
pg. 87

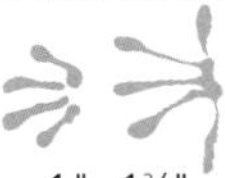
1" 1⅜"

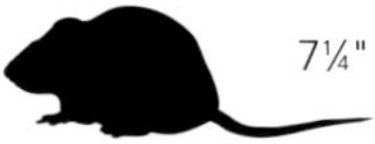
7¼"

Hispid Cotton Rat
pg. 91

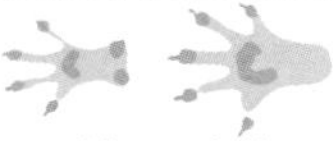
1" 1½"

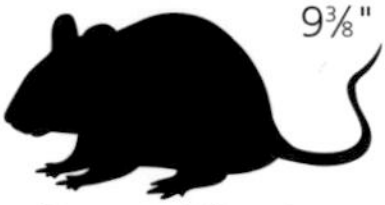
9⅜"

Eastern Woodrat
pg. 99

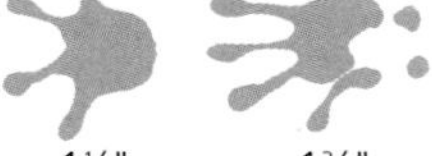
1¼" 1¾"

Body length measurements
do not include tail.

Average size of the smallest and
largest of this group compared to
an 8" hand.

Silhouettes are in proportion
to each other by average body
length.

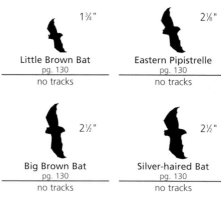

1¾"

Little Brown Bat
pg. 130
no tracks

2⅛"

Eastern Pipistrelle
pg. 130
no tracks

2½"

Big Brown Bat
pg. 130
no tracks

2½"

Silver-haired Bat
pg. 130
no tracks

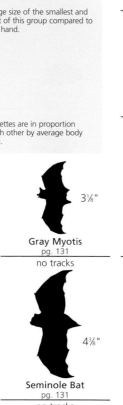

3⅛"

Gray Myotis
pg. 131
no tracks

3⅛"

Little Mastiff Bat
pg. 131
no tracks

3½"

Wagner's Bonneted Bat
pg. 131
no tracks

4⅜"

Seminole Bat
pg. 131
no tracks

Evening Bat
pg. 130
no tracks
2¼"

Northern Myotis
pg. 130
no tracks
2¼"

Brazilian Free-tailed Bat
pg. 127
no tracks
2⅜"

Eastern Red Bat
pg. 131
no tracks
2½"

Indiana Bat
pg. 131
no tracks
2⅝"

Hoary Bat
pg. 131
no tracks
3"

Southeastern Bat
pg. 131
no tracks
3½"

Rafinesque's Big-eared Bat pg. 131
no tracks
4"

Northern Yellow Bat
pg. 131
no tracks
4¼"

Body length measurements do not include tail.

Average size of the smallest and largest of this group compared to a 6' human.

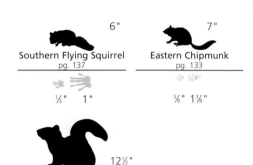

6"

Southern Flying Squirrel
pg. 137

½"   1"

7"

Eastern Chipmunk
pg. 133

⅝"   1⅜"

12½"

Fox Squirrel
pg. 149

1½"   2⅞"

Body length measurements do not include tail.

Average size of the smallest and largest of this group compared to a 6' human.

Silhouettes are in proportion by average body length. Tracks are in proportion by average largest foot. Front track is on the left and hind is on the right.

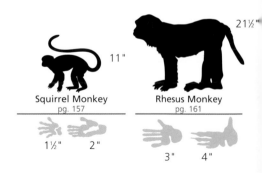

11"

Squirrel Monkey
pg. 157

1½"   2"

21½"

Rhesus Monkey
pg. 161

3"   4"

8½"

Eastern Gray Squirrel
pg. 141

1"   2¼"

9¾"

Red-bellied Squirrel
pg. 145

1"   2¾"

11"

**Southeastern Pocket
Gopher** pg. 153

1¼"   ¾"

19

Body length measurements do not include tail.

Average size of the smallest and largest of this group compared to a 6' human.

Silhouettes are in proportion by average body length. Tracks are in proportion by average largest foot. Front track is on the left and hind is on the right.

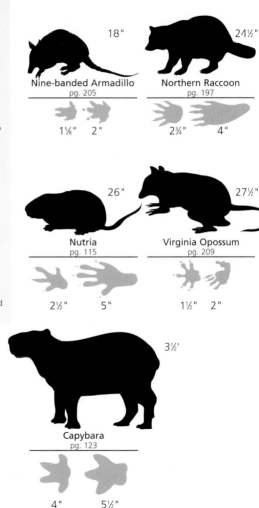

18"

Nine-banded Armadillo
pg. 205

1⅝"   2"

24½"

Northern Raccoon
pg. 197

2¾"   4"

26"

Nutria
pg. 115

2½"   5"

27½"

Virginia Opossum
pg. 209

1½"   2"

3½'

Capybara
pg. 123

4"   5½"

20

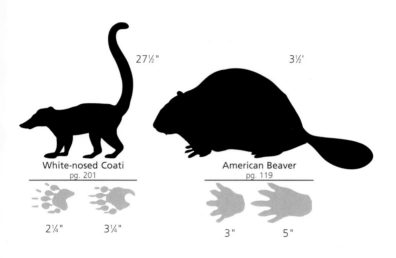

27½"

3½'

White-nosed Coati
pg. 201

American Beaver
pg. 119

2¼"   3¼"

3"   5"

Body length measurements
do not include tail.

Average size of the smallest and
largest of this group compared to
a 6' human.

Marsh Rabbit
pg. 165

15"

½"   3¾"

Eastern Cottontail
pg. 169

16"

1"   3½"

Body length measurements
do not include tail.

Average size of the smallest and
largest of this group compared to
a 6' human.

Long-tailed Weasel
pg. 177

12"

¾"   ⅞"

Eastern Spotted Skunk
pg. 189

14"

1"   1¼"

Northern River Otter
pg. 185

36"

3⅜"   3½"

Silhouettes are in proportion by
average body length. Tracks are
in proportion by average largest
foot. Front track is on the left and
hind is on the right.

Black-tailed Jackrabbit
pg. 173

21"

1"   4¾"

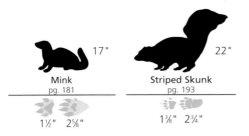

Mink
pg. 181

17"

1½"   2⅝"

Striped Skunk
pg. 193

22"

1⅜"   2¾"

Body length measurements do not include tail.

Average size of the smallest and largest of this group compared to a 6' human.

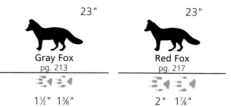

23"
Gray Fox
pg. 213

1½" 1⅜"

23"
Red Fox
pg. 217

2" 1⅞"

Body length measurements do not include tail.

Average size of the smallest and largest of this group compared to a 6' human.

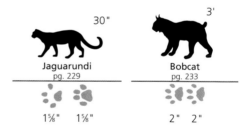

30"
Jaguarundi
pg. 229

1⅝" 1⅝"

3'
Bobcat
pg. 233

2" 2"

Silhouettes are in proportion by average body length. Tracks are in proportion by average largest foot. Front track is on the left and hind is on the right.

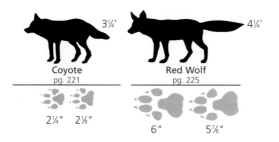

Coyote
pg. 221

2¼"   2⅛"

Red Wolf
pg. 225

6"   5⅞"

3¼'

4¼'

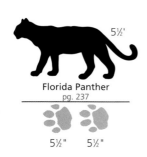

Florida Panther
pg. 237

5½"   5½"

5½'

Body length measurements
do not include tail.

Average size of the smallest and
largest of this group compared to
a 6' human.

2½'

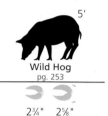

Key Deer
pg. 241

1" ⅞"

5'

Wild Hog
pg. 253

2¾" 2⅝"

10'

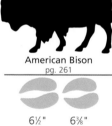

American Bison
pg. 261

6½" 6⅜"

Silhouettes are in proportion by
average body length. Tracks are
in proportion by average largest
foot. Front track is on the left and
hind is on the right.

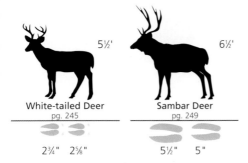

White-tailed Deer
pg. 245

2¾"   2⅝"

Sambar Deer
pg. 249

5½"   5"

5½'

6½'

Body length measurements do not include tail.

Average size of bear compared to a 6' human.

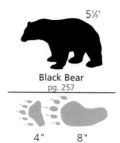

5¼'

Black Bear
pg. 257

4"   8"

Body length measurements include the tail.

Average size of the smallest and largest of this group compared to a 6' human.

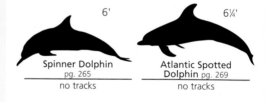

6'

Spinner Dolphin
pg. 265
no tracks

6¼'

Atlantic Spotted Dolphin pg. 269
no tracks

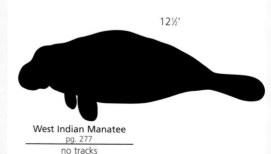

12½'

West Indian Manatee
pg. 277
no tracks

Silhouettes are in proportion by average body length. Tracks are in proportion by average largest foot. Front track is on the left and hind is on the right.

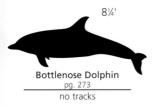

8¼'

Bottlenose Dolphin
pg. 273
no tracks

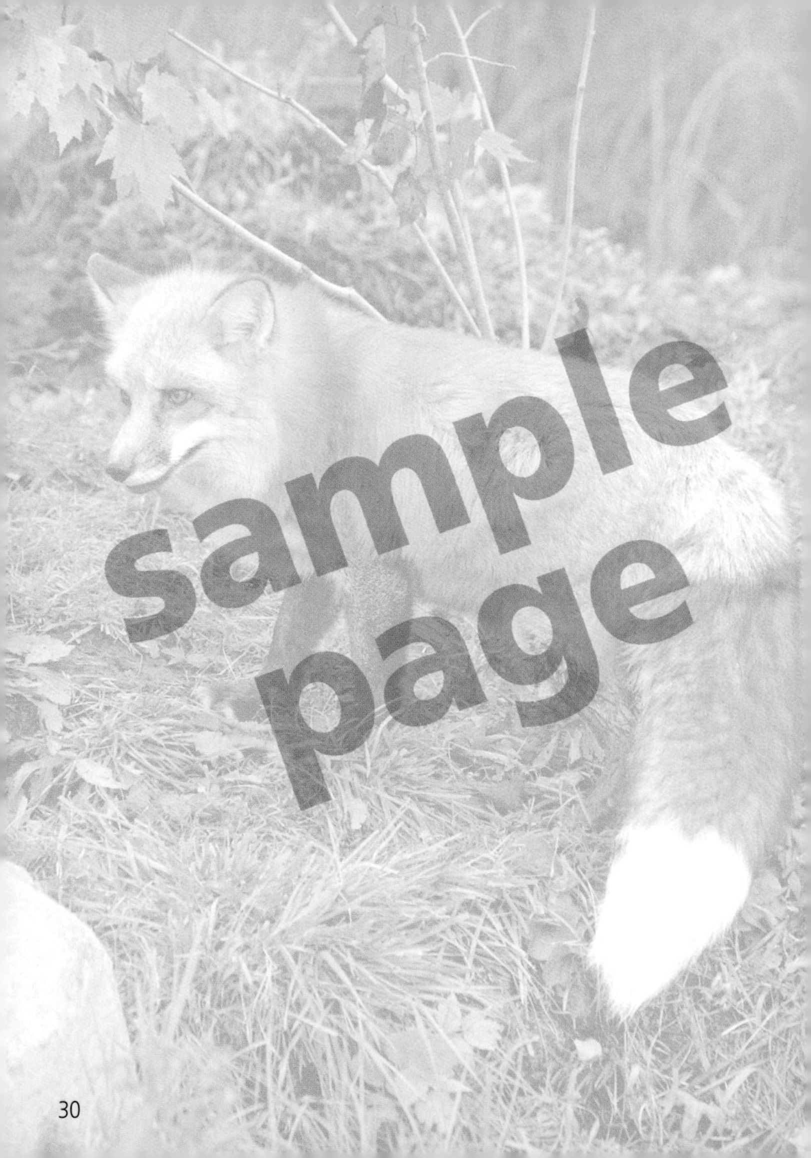

FORMER
RANGE

Family: common family name (scientific family name)

Size: (L) average length or range of length of body from head to rump; for marine, range of length from head to tail; (T) average length or range of length of tail; (H) average height or range of height to top of back

Weight: average weight or range of weight; may include (M) male and (F) female weights

Description: brief description of the mammal; may include color morphs, seasonal variations or differences between male and female

Origin/Age: native or non-native to Florida or the waters off the coast; average life span in the wild

Compare: notes about other species that look similar and the pages on which they can be found; may include extra information to help identify

Habitat: environment where the animal is seen (e.g., wetlands, scrublands, fields, prairies, forests)

Home: description of nest, burrow or den; may include other related information

Food: herbivore, carnivore, insectivore, omnivore or ichthyophagous; what the animal eats most of the time; may include other related information

Sounds: vocalization or other noises the animal creates; may include variant sounds or other information

Breeding: mating season; length of gestation

Young: number of offspring born per year and when; may include description or birth weight

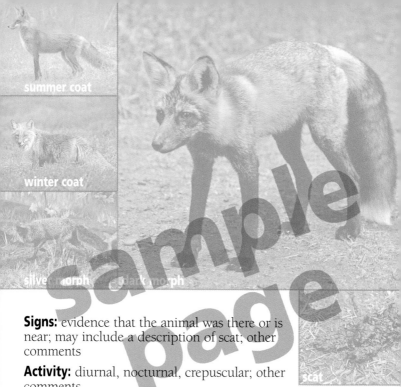

summer coat

winter coat

silver morph   dark morph

scat

Signs: evidence that the animal was there or is near; may include a description of scat; other comments

Activity: diurnal, nocturnal, crepuscular; other comments

Tracks: forepaw and hind paw or hoof size and shape, largest size first; pattern of tracks; description of prints, which may include tail drag mark or stride; other comments

Tracks and Pattern

Stan's Notes: Interesting gee-whiz natural history information. This can be something to look or listen for, or something to help positively identify the animal such as remarkable features. May include additional photos to illustrate juveniles, nests, unique behaviors and other key characteristics.

den entrance

kits

Similar species on next page (bat species only)

Least Shrew
Cryptotis parva

Family: Shrews (Soricidae)

Size: L 1½-2¼" (4-5.5 cm); T ½-¾" (1-2 cm)

Weight: ⅛-¼ oz. (4-7 g)

Description: Mostly brown above, but fur can be gray. Lighter belly. Pointed snout. Tiny dark eyes. Short tail, never more than twice as long as the hind foot. Small pink feet. Ears barely visible.

Origin/Age: native; 1-2 years

Compare: Smaller than the Southern Short-tailed Shrew (pg. 43), which has a tail about the same length, but a larger body and is darker overall. Smaller than the Southeastern Shrew (pg. 39) and has a shorter tail.

Habitat: fields, grasslands, meadows, shrubby areas

Home: chamber in an underground burrow, nest made with dried leaves and grasses

Food: insectivore, carnivore; beetles, crickets, spiders, grasshoppers, slugs, earthworms, snails, small mammals

Sounds: inconsequential; sharp squeaks and high-pitched whistles can be heard from up to 2' (61 cm) away

Breeding: Mar-Nov mating; 21-23 days gestation

Young: 1-6 offspring several times per year; born naked with eyes closed, weaned at about 3 weeks

Signs: partially eaten insects near the burrow entrance; extremely tiny, dark scat, widely scattered

Activity: nocturnal, diurnal; may be more active during the day in summer, when nights are shorter

Tracks: hind paw ¼-½" (.6-1 cm) long, forepaw slightly smaller; 1 set of 4 tracks, but prints are so close together they appear to be 1 track; 4 prints together are 1 square inch (6.5 sq. cm), often lacks a tail drag mark due to its short tail

Stan's Notes: One of Florida's least studied shrew species, thus not much is known about its biology. Range in the United States is widespread, from Minnesota down to Texas, east to Florida and up the entire East coast, excluding New England.

Sometimes called Bee Shrew because it supposedly lives in beehives; however, this has never been studied or widely reported and may be a reference to the animal's small size. It has been reported to take up residency in a beehive while eating the bees that occupy it.

Hunts for invertebrates by probing through leaf litter with its nose, smelling for prey. Often feeds only on the internal organs of large insects. Subdues prey by capturing and biting off the head, which makes it easier to get to internal organs. Like other shrews, it eats nearly its own body weight in food each day. When food is abundant it will cache some for later consumption.

While most other shrew species are solitary, Least Shrew appears to be more social, with many individuals sharing one nest. It is thought that owls, particularly Barn Owls, are its major predators. In one study, Least Shrews made up 41 percent of the diet of one Barn Owl pair. In another pair, Least Shrews made up 73 percent of the diet.

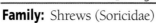

Southeastern Shrew
Sorex longirostris

Family: Shrews (Soricidae)

Size: L 2-3" (5-7.5 cm); T 1-1¼" (2.5-3 cm)

Weight: ¹⁄₁₆-⅛ oz. (2-4 g)

Description: Overall reddish brown with a gray belly. A very long, pointed and nearly naked snout. Tiny dark eyes. Ears slightly visible. Short bicolored tail, reddish brown above and lighter below with a short tuft at the tip.

Origin/Age: native; 1-2 years

Compare: Southern Short-tailed Shrew (pg. 43) is larger and darker in color overall. Least Shrew (pg. 35) is slightly smaller and has a shorter tail.

Habitat: wet meadows, pine forests, plantations, fields, wetlands, moist deciduous forests

Home: nest, 4-6" (10-15 cm) wide, made of leaves and grasses, under a log or rock, near wetlands

Food: insectivore, carnivore; insects, ants, slugs, spiders, earthworms, small mammals such as mice

Sounds: inconsequential; sharp squeaks and high-pitched whistles, gives a series of clicks and twitters

Breeding: spring to autumn mating; 18 days gestation

Young: 2-6 offspring 2-3 times per year; young are born naked with eyes closed, eyes open at 17-19 days, weaned at about 20 days, on their own within days of being weaned

Signs: tiny tunnels or runways in freshly dug soil; shrew is rarely, if ever, seen

Activity: diurnal, nocturnal; active year-round

Tracks: hind paw ½" (1 cm) long, forepaw slightly smaller; 1 set of 4 tracks, but prints are so close together they look like 1 track; 4 prints together are 1 square inch (6.5 sq. cm), sometimes has a slight tail drag mark

Stan's Notes: This secretive, solitary animal is rarely seen due to its underground lifestyle. Range extends from southern Illinois and Missouri east to the Maryland coast and south to central Florida. Not very common in Florida.

Not a well-studied mammal, but a good species to have around because it eats many insects and spiders. A discrete animal that does not pose problems for people. Due to the damp nature of soils in Florida, there are not a lot of digging animals such as shrews. Consequently, shrews are often found in woodpiles and under old wooden buildings that have fallen down.

Shrews have poor vision and hold their eyes shut tightly when burrowing underground. They communicate with each other by a series of clicks and twitters and also through echolocation, a type of communication that is not well understood.

Shrews are fierce predators, but they are also near the bottom of the food chain. They are eaten by many larger predators, from bobcats to coyotes to a whole host of avian predators such as owls, hawks and eagles.

Also called Bachman's Shrew in honor of naturalist John Bachman, who discovered the species in 1837. The genus *Sorex* is Latin for "shrew" or "mouse." The species *longirostris* is from the Latin word *longus*, meaning "long" and "rostrum," referring to its snout. Taken together, it is a shrew with a long snout, which best describes the long, nearly naked snout.

Southern Short-tailed Shrew
Blarina carolinensis

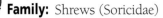

Family: Shrews (Soricidae)

Size: L 3-4" (7.5-10 cm); T ¾-1" (2-2.5 cm)

Weight: ⅛-¾ oz. (4-21 g)

Description: Overall dark to slate gray, with a short, nearly naked tail. Long pointed snout. Small pink feet. Tiny dark eyes, usually not noticed. Ears barely visible. Younger individuals are often darker.

Origin/Age: native; 1-2 years

Compare: More common than the Least Shrew (pg. 35), which is smaller and grayer. Larger than the Southeastern Shrew (pg. 39), which has a naked snout and longer tail.

Habitat: wide variety of habitats such as moist deciduous woodlands, coniferous forests, fields, meadows, yards and gardens

Home: bulky nest, 6-10" (15-25 cm) wide, made from dried grasses and leaves, usually beneath a log or rock or inside a rotting stump

Food: insectivore; beetles, earthworms, snails, spiders, mice, voles, toads, subterranean fungi

Sounds: inconsequential; sharp squeaks and high-pitched whistles can be heard up to 10' (3 m) away

Breeding: Mar-Jun and Sep-Nov mating; 21-22 days gestation

Young: 2-6 offspring twice per year; born only as large as a honeybee, naked with eyes closed, weaned after about 2 days

Signs: well-worn inch-wide runways or tunnels through grass or sand, piles of snail shells and insect parts under a log, fallen tree bark or other shelter

Activity: diurnal, nocturnal; active year-round

Tracks: hind paw ⅜-½" (.9-1 cm) long, forepaw slightly smaller; continuous grooves in sand or runways in lawns with no distinct prints; continuous grooves and runways are due to its low-slung body and short legs, which do not allow it to hop or jump

Stan's Notes: One of three shrew species in Florida and by far the most common. Found across the state, with a subspecies seen in southwestern Florida. Although widespread, shrews in Florida are hard to find and observe. Populations can climb to very high and then drop suddenly, making the animal more abundant one year and absent the next.

Very similar to its northern cousin, Northern Short-tailed Shrew (not shown). Most of what is known about the Southern Short-tailed comes from the observations of the Northern.

This is a unique animal because it is the only North American mammal that produces a poisonous saliva. It cannot inject the poison, but chews it into a wound. The poison paralyzes small prey such as mice; can cause tingling and numbness in people.

A solitary shrew. Excavates tunnels underground or runways just below leaf litter, where it patrols for food. Ears and eyes function, but usually go unnoticed because they are so small. Finds most of its prey by smell and feel. Uses ultrasonic clicks (echolocation) to detect objects in dark tunnels, much like a bat. Hunts for short periods of 3-5 minutes, then rests for 20-30 minutes. Consumes half its own weight in food every day. Caches food underground, returning often to eat and replenish the supply. Many cannot live more than 24-48 hours in captivity without food and water. They have a heart rate of one thousand beats per minute.

The male will scent mark its territory with urine, feces or oily secretions from glands near the base of the tail. Marking territory helps reduce the chance of a fatal encounter since rival neighbors will sometimes fight each other to death. Scent marking also advertises social status, helps to attract mates and, as an added benefit, may deter predators that find the glands distasteful.

The female is ready to reproduce as early as 46 days. Mates may stay together for long periods, maybe even for life. Young are born with adult teeth and can chew food right away.

Star-nosed Mole
Condylura cristata

Family: Moles (Talpidae)

Size: L 3-7" (7.5-18 cm); T ¾-1¼" (2-3 cm)

Weight: 1-2½ oz. (28-71 g)

Description: Fur is dark gray to nearly black. Twenty or more thin, fleshy pink projections on nose in a circular pattern. Short legs. Extremely large front feet with long, well-defined claws. A long tail with sparse hair, constricted at the base. Invisible ears. Pinpoint eyes, often hidden.

Origin/Age: native; 1-2 years

Compare: Spends more of its time above the ground than the Eastern Mole (pg. 51). Look for large, fleshy pink projections on the nose to help identify.

Habitat: wet woodlands, moist fields, wetlands, ponds, lakes, streams

Home: burrow, beneath a log or fallen tree, nest is lined with dead leaves and grasses during summer, in a chamber connected to a tunnel system below the frost line during winter, separate chambers for giving birth and raising young

Food: insectivore, carnivore; insects, slugs, earthworms, crustaceans, fish

Sounds: inconsequential; rarely, if ever, heard

Breeding: Apr-May mating; 35-45 days gestation; starts to breed at 10 months

Young: 3-7 (average 5) offspring once per year in April or May, some born as late as August; born naked, helpless, with the "star" nose enclosed in a thin translucent membrane and eyes closed

47

Signs: ridges as a result of tunneling near the surface of soil, mounds of fresh soil (molehills) pushed up during construction of tunnels, runways on the surface leading to and from holes in the ground

Activity: diurnal, nocturnal; active year-round, spends less time underground than other moles

Tracks: hind paw 1" (2.5 cm) long with 5 toes, forepaw 1½" (4 cm) long with 5 toes; individual tracks are indistinguishable and create a single groove with claw marks, sometimes has a tail drag mark

Stan's Notes: An easily recognizable mole in the state, but not very common and seen only in isolated locations in northern Florida. Its fleshy, tentacle-like pink nose and long tail make it easy to identify. Nose projections (nasal rays) are presumably used to feel for worms in the darkness underground. Recent studies have indicated they contain highly sensitive tactile organs called Eimer's organs, believed to detect electrical fields given by prey. It is also thought that nasal rays help a mole manipulate objects such as food during capturing and eating. The tail fattens during spring and summer, presumably as an energy store for the breeding season and coming winter, thickening as a result of fat deposition. Main prey are earthworms and insects.

Eyes are tiny and probably useful only to detect light. Digs less powerfully than the more common Eastern Mole (pg. 51), but is a very good swimmer. Can dive after aquatic animals, including fish. Propels itself underwater by moving its feet and tail for extra propulsion. Also a good tunneler, with tunnels often opening out underwater. Has additional aboveground paths or "runs."

Often gregarious and even colonial. Active under snow and even beneath the ice of frozen lakes and streams. Babies grow quickly, leaving nests and mothers at 3-4 weeks.

The genus name *Condylura* is Greek and means "knobby tail," referring to one of the first and, unfortunately, inaccurate drawings of this animal showing a bumpy or knobby tail, much like a string of beads. The species name *cristata* is Latin for "crest" or "tuft" and refers to the star-shaped pattern of projections on the nose. There are six other mole species north of Mexico in North America.

Eastern Mole
Scalopus aquaticus

Family: Moles (Talpidae)

Size: L 4-7" (10-18 cm); T ¾-1¼" (2-3 cm)

Weight: 3-5 oz. (85-142 g)

Description: Short silky fur, dark brown to gray with a silver sheen. Long pointed snout. Very large, naked front feet, more wide than long and resembling human hands with palms turned outward. Very short, nearly naked tail. Pinpoint eyes, frequently hidden by fur. Male slightly larger than female.

Origin/Age: native; 1-2 years

Compare: A unique-looking animal with extremely short legs, no visible eyes, a short tail and large, human-like pink hands for paws. Much smaller than the Southeastern Pocket Gopher (pg. 153), which has obvious eyes and a longer tail.

Habitat: dry grassy areas, fields, lawns, gardens, loose well-drained soils

Home: burrow, tunnels usually are 4-20" (10-50 cm) underground in summer, deeper tunnels below the frost line during winter, nest is in a chamber connected to a tunnel, with separate chambers for giving birth and raising young

Food: insectivore, herbivore; insects, grubs, roots, earthworms

Sounds: inconsequential; rarely, if ever, heard

Breeding: Feb-Mar mating; 32-42 days gestation

Young: 2-6 offspring once per year in early spring; born naked with eyes closed, weaned at 30-40 days, leaves nest chamber when weaned

tail

Signs: ridges of soil from tunnel construction just below the surface of the ground, sometimes small piles of soil on the ground (molehills) from digging deeper permanent tunnels

Activity: diurnal, nocturnal; active year-round, does not appear to time its activities with the rising and setting of the sun

Tracks: hind paw ⅝" (1.5 cm) long with 5 toes, forepaw 1½" (4 cm) long with 5 toes; individual tracks are indistinguishable and create a single groove with claw marks, sometimes has a tail drag mark; spends almost all of its time in its underground tunnel system, so tracks are rarely seen

Stan's Notes: The first time this animal was described in records was when a drowned mole was found in a well. It was presumed, in error, to be aquatic; hence the Latin species name *aquaticus,* which also refers to the slight webbing between its toes. This is the most subterranean mammal in Florida, spending 99 percent of its life underground. Also called Common Mole or just Mole.

The Eastern Mole has no external ears. Its tiny eyes are covered with skin and detect light only, not shapes or colors. It has large white teeth, unlike the shrews, which have chestnut or tan teeth. Uses its very sensitive, flexible snout to find food by smelling and sensing vibrations with its whiskers. The nap of its short fur can lie forward or backward, making it easier to travel in either direction in tight tunnels. A narrow pelvis allows it to somersault often and reverse its heading.

Excavates its own tunnel system. Uses its front feet to dig while pushing loosened soil back and out of the way with its hind feet. Able to dig 12 inches (30 cm) per minute in loose soil. Digging and tunneling is beneficial to the environment; it aerates the soil and allows moisture to penetrate deeper into the ground.

Searches for subterranean insects, earthworms, some plant roots and other food in temporary tunnels, usually located just below the surface of the ground. Deeper permanent tunnels are used for living, nesting and depositing waste. Will move to even deeper tunnels below the frost line during winter.

The male will seek out a female in her tunnel to mate during late winter. It is thought that a female rarely leaves her tunnel system except when a young female leaves the tunnels of her mother to establish her own.

Unlike most other small mammals, it reproduces only once each year. Not preyed upon as heavily due to its burrowing (fossorial) life, so does not need to reproduce often.

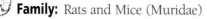

Eastern Harvest Mouse
Reithrodontomys humulis

Family: Rats and Mice (Muridae)

Size: L 2¼-2¾" (5.5-7 cm); T 2-2¼" (5-5.5 cm)

Weight: ¼-⅜ oz. (7-11 g)

Description: Overall dark brown fur, nearly black down the center of back and reddish brown on the sides. Grayish white underbelly. Large dark ears and large eyes. Tail is thin, nearly naked, somewhat bicolored, not tufted and equal to the length of the head and body combined. Gray or nearly white feet. Grooved front teeth (upper incisors).

Origin/Age: native; 1-2 years

Compare: House Mouse (pg. 63) is larger and overall gray. Unlike the House, Eastern Harvest usually does not enter buildings. Smaller than Golden Mouse (pg. 67), which is overall golden brown.

Habitat: wet grassy areas, fields, roadsides, sedge patches, wetlands

Home: underground burrow with multiple chambers, aboveground ball-shaped nest made of dried grass, 5-6" (13-15 cm) diameter, occasionally low in a shrub or small tree or attached to grass stems, often in an old bird nest

Food: herbivore, insectivore; seeds, vegetation, fruit, fresh green shoots in spring, insects

Sounds: inconsequential; high-pitched trilling call

Breeding: year-round mating; 21-22 days gestation

Young: 3-5 (average 4) pups up to 4 times per year; born naked with eyes closed, weighing about ½ oz. (14 g)

55

Signs: surface runways, ball-shaped nest made of dried grass on the ground, most obvious after a field or grassland fire, nest is sometimes attached to grass stems or in a small tree or shrub

Activity: mostly nocturnal; active year-round, often huddles in nest during the day with other members of its family

Tracks: hind paw ½" (1 cm) long with 5 toes, forepaw ⅛" (.3 cm) long with 4 toes; sometimes has a tail drag mark

Stan's Notes: The smallest of harvest mice, ranging from Florida to Texas up the East coast to Maryland and across to the southern tip of Illinois. It harvests dried grass to build a large softball-sized nest, hence the common name. Known to use the nest of a bird as a base to build a ball nest of dried grass. Uses underground burrows, but may use more than one nest in its home range, including one or two in shrubs. Uses the runways and burrows of other animals such as pocket gophers and voles.

Considered to be a good mouse to have around because it feeds heavily on weed seeds. Stores many seeds in caches underground. A big climber, jumping into trees and shrubs and scurrying about among the branches. Tolerant of one another and not territorial. Rarely enters homes or other buildings.

A female usually has up to four litters per season. However, it has been reported that a captive female harvest mouse reproduced as many as 14 times, giving birth to a total of 58 young.

The Eastern and other harvest mice species have been classified in *Reithrodontomys*, a genus separate from other small mice. One way to identify a harvest mouse is by the groove front-and-center in its upper incisor teeth, which other small mice lack. In addition, the harvest mouse lacks the fur-lined cheek pouches of pocket mice. Although some pocket mice species have grooved incisors like those of harvest mice, this is not a feature that a casual observer will see.

Can be extremely abundant where it occurs, often with very high population densities. Can survive a long time without drinking free-standing water. Presumably obtains all of its water needs through the diet.

Oldfield Mouse
Peromyscus polionotus

Family: Rats and Mice (Muridae)

Size: L 2½-3" (6-7.5 cm); T 1¾-2" (4.5-5 cm)

Weight: ¼-½ oz. (7-14 g)

Description: Overall tan to light gray with a white chin, chest, belly, legs and feet. Bicolored tail, with the same colors as the body, but sparsely furred, lacking a tuft and much shorter than the length of the head and body. Large, round naked ears.

Origin/Age: native; 6 months to 2 years

Compare: The closer to the coast, the lighter gray the fur. The Cotton Mouse (pg. 71) and Florida Mouse (pg. 75) are both larger and darker, with longer tails. Eastern Harvest Mouse (pg. 55) is darker and has a gray belly and grooved upper incisors.

Habitat: old fields, vacant farms, beaches, sand dunes, dry scrub

Home: nest in underground tunnels that it excavates, almost always nests in sandy soils to facilitate the extensive burrowing

Food: herbivore, insectivore; seeds, vegetation, fruit, nuts, insects

Sounds: inconsequential

Breeding: year-round mating; 22-24 days gestation

Young: 3-5 pups up to 3-4 times per year; born with eyes and ears closed, opening 13-14 days later

59

Beach

Signs: stockpiles of seeds in underground nest chambers, strong smell of urine in the areas it often visits; small, hard black scat the size of a pinhead

Activity: nocturnal

Tracks: hind paw ¾" (2 cm) long with 5 toes, forepaw ⅝" (1.5 cm) long with 4 toes; 1 set of 4 tracks; sometimes has a tail drag mark

Stan's Notes: A rare mouse of old fields, abandoned farms and homesteads. Also in beaches and sand dunes along the coast.

The Oldfield Mouse is by far the lightest colored mouse species in Florida. A subspecies of Oldfield Mouse, often called Beach Mouse, is even lighter in color. The closer to the coast and sandier the habitat, the lighter gray the mouse appears, presumably to blend in better with lighter, sandy environments. Many islands along the northern Gulf coast and Atlantic coast have their own unique subspecies. Some of these subspecies are so light in color that they appear to be almost entirely white. Both the Oldfield Mouse and Beach Mouse are very uncommon due to habitat loss.

Highly nocturnal, coming out only at night to feed on seeds and insects. Stores large amounts of seed in its burrow. Most tunnels are only 12-36 inches (30-91 cm) beneath the ground surface. Each tunnel has a main entrance and an escape tunnel. A small amount of sand usually marks the entrance of the main tunnel.

Adult females are slightly larger than adult males. The species is monogamous, with pairs staying together for their entire life. Life span is only 6 months to 2 years. Breeds year-round in Florida, but mating declines slightly during the summer months. Never leaves its small home territory.

Beneficial to have around because it eats many weed seeds and insects. It is also food for many predator species such as hawks, owls, snakes, foxes and more.

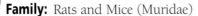

House Mouse
Mus musculus

Family: Rats and Mice (Muridae)

Size: L 2½-4" (6-10 cm); T 2-4" (5-10 cm)

Weight: ½-¾ oz. (14-21 g)

Description: Gray to light brown above, slightly lighter gray below. Large ears. Tail is gray above, naked and nearly the same length as the body.

Origin/Age: non-native; 1-2 years

Compare: One of the smaller mouse species in Florida, making it easy to identify. The Eastern Harvest Mouse (pg. 55) is smaller, overall brown and usually does not enter buildings.

Habitat: houses, buildings, cultivated fields

Home: nest with a hollow center, mass of plant or man-made material such as paper or insulation

Food: herbivore, insectivore; seeds, vegetation, fruit, nuts, insects

Sounds: inconsequential; scampering or scratching can be heard

Breeding: Mar-Oct mating; 18-21 days gestation

Young: 2-15 pups 3-4 times per year; born naked with eyes closed

Signs: strong smell of urine in the areas it often visits; small, hard black droppings the size of a pinhead

Activity: nocturnal; active year-round

Tracks: hind paw ½" (1 cm) long with 5 toes, forepaw ¼" (.6 cm) long with 4 toes; 1 set of 4 tracks; sometimes has a tail drag mark

scat

Stan's Notes: One of several non-native mammals in the state. Originally from central Asia, it was inadvertently introduced into North America by Spanish ships that landed in the New World in the sixteenth century.

Uncommon in undisturbed areas and frequently associated with people. Competes effectively with and often displaces native mice and voles, making it an unwanted species. Especially not wanted in homes since it is known to carry disease, damage structures and contaminate food. Must live in a heated dwelling such as a barn or home since it cannot tolerate cold or survive a northern winter. However, it thrives in fields in southern states without the assistance of protective structures.

White mice used in laboratory experiments are bred from albino mice of this species. The species name *musculus* comes from the Sanskrit word *musha*, meaning "thief," and refers to its habit of gathering or "stealing" large quantities of food from homes. Will chew just about anything. It even gnaws holes in wood, giving rise to the stereotypical baseboard mouse hole seen in cartoons.

Lives in small to large groups and tolerates overpopulation well. Shares nests, burrows and tunnels with others of its species and performs mutual grooming. While other mouse species become carnivorous when there is overcrowding, a female House Mouse will simply reproduce less often or part of the group will migrate to a new location.

Golden Mouse
Ochrotomys nuttalli

Family: Rats and Mice (Muridae)

Size: L 3½-4" (9-10 cm); T 3-3½" (7.5-9 cm)

Weight: ¾-1 oz. (21-28 g)

Description: Golden brown back, sometimes tinged yellow on the sides. Creamy white chin and belly. Bicolored tail, matching the color of the body and the same length as the head and body. Tail sparsely haired and semiprehensile. Large, round naked ears.

Origin/Age: native; 1-2 years

Compare: Eastern Harvest Mouse (pg. 55) is much darker and has a shorter tail. Slightly smaller than the Cotton Mouse (pg. 71), which is dark brown to almost black. Golden has a unique color and is one of the easiest mice to identify by this alone.

Habitat: trees, dense tangles of shrubs, oak woods, forests

Home: nest, loose round mass of plant material (such as Spanish moss) with a hollow center, lined with animal hair, milkweed silk or other soft material, 3-30' (.9-9.1 m) above the ground in thick vegetation or Spanish moss, sometimes on the ground; leaves nest when it is soaked with urine

Food: herbivore; seeds, fruit, nuts; also some insects

Sounds: inconsequential; scratching or scampering

Breeding: year-round mating; 22-23 days gestation

Young: 2-5 pups up to 3-4 or more times per year; reddish brown, born with eyes and ears closed, opening 11-14 days later, weaned at 3 weeks, sexually mature at 1-2 months

Signs: globular nests in trees, especially in Spanish moss, some nests are made of pine needles, located in thick tangles of vines, briers or shrubs, sometimes a round nest is constructed in an old bird nest

Activity: nocturnal

Tracks: hind paw ¾" (2 cm) long with 5 toes, forepaw ½" (1 cm) long with 4 toes; 1 set of 4 tracks; spends much of its time in trees (semiarboreal), making tracks uncommon

Stan's Notes: A unique-looking mouse and one of the easiest to identify simply by its color. Also unique because it climbs trees (semiarboreal) and builds its nest off the ground.

A common mouse of southeastern states, ranging from southern Illinois to Louisiana, east to central Florida and up to coastal Virginia. Prefers dense woodlands with abundant cover. Climbs trees, scampering across tree branches, using its tail for balance. Some report that the tail tip is used to help grip (semiprehensile).

Nests mainly in trees, building large ball-shaped nests of plant material such as Spanish moss, pine needles and such. Lines the nest with soft plant material or animal fur. Builds several nests within easy scampering distance. Most are above the surface of the ground; some are on the ground. Has been known to use an old bird nest as a base to make its own nesting chamber. Males and females share the nest until the young are born. After their birth, males no longer enters the nest.

Eats mainly seeds, collecting fruit and seeds from many kinds of plants such as sumac, greenbrier, cherry and even poison ivy. It has specialized internal cheek pouches in which it carries seeds back to feeding platforms in the tree. These are usually areas with flattened vegetation where the mouse will sit and eat what it gathered in the safety of the thick vegetation on the ground.

In other parts of the country, this mouse breeds seasonally. In Florida it is a year-round breeder, with females giving birth many times each year.

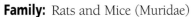

Cotton Mouse
Peromyscus gossypinus

Family: Rats and Mice (Muridae)

Size: L 3¾-4¼" (9.5-10.5 cm); T 3-3½" (7.5-9 cm)

Weight: ¾-1½ oz. (21-43 g)

Description: Overall reddish brown, nearly black on center of back, gradually browner on sides. White chest, belly, legs and feet. Bicolored tail, dark brown above, white below, shorter than head and body. Large bulging eyes. Large, round naked ears. Each hind foot has 6 pads (tubercles) on the sole.

Origin/Age: native; 6 months to 1 year

Compare: Oldfield Mouse (pg. 59) is overall gray, with a short tail. Florida Mouse (pg. 75) has red on its sides, a red brown back and 5 pads on hind feet.

Habitat: wide variety such as woodlands, fields, swamps, river bottoms, sand dunes, buildings

Home: nest, loose round mass of plant material with a hollow center, lined with cotton, animal hair, milkweed silk or other soft material, under a log or other shelter such as a tortoise burrow, sometimes inside a log or standing tree; abandons nest when soiled with urine and builds another

Food: omnivore; seeds, vegetation, fruit, nuts, insects

Sounds: inconsequential; scratching or scampering can be heard, high-pitched squeak if around other mice

Breeding: year-round, but mainly Mar-Oct mating; 22-23 days gestation

Young: 4-7 pups up to 3-4 times per year; all gray when very young, dull brown after 40-50 days, reddish brown in a couple months

71

Signs: stockpiles of seeds near nest, strong smell of urine in the areas it often visits; small, hard black scat the size of a pinhead

Activity: nocturnal

Tracks: hind paw 1" (2.5 cm) long with 5 toes, forepaw ¾" (2 cm) long with 4 toes; 1 set of 4 tracks; sometimes has a tail drag mark

Stan's Notes: Most likely the most common small mammal in Florida. Found in a wide variety of habitats throughout the entire state. Very closely related to White-footed Mouse (not shown) of northern states. Like other mice, Cotton Mouse is an important part of the ecosystem, being prey for many animals such as foxes, coyotes, hawks, owls and more. It also helps move seeds around, which sprout later and grow.

The range extends from Florida up the eastern coast to Virginia, west to the southern tip of Illinois and southwest to the middle of Texas. Cotton Mouse is a great swimmer. It is also an excellent climber, often climbing trees to find seeds. Uses its tail to help maintain balance when climbing. Enjoys a variety of food, about 50 percent seed and 50 percent animal and insect.

The species name *gossypinus* comes from the Latin and means "cotton." However, it doesn't live in cotton fields, as the common name suggests. Instead, it gathers cotton to line its nest. Enters homes in fall for shelter and food, but not as much as the House Mouse (pg. 63) and Norway Rat (pg. 95).

The Cotton Mouse has six bumps, called tubercles, on the sole of each rear foot. Noting the number of tubercles is a good way to help distinguish it from the Florida Mouse (pg. 75), which has only five tubercles on each hind foot.

The Key Largo Cotton Mouse, a rare subspecies of Cotton Mouse, occurs only on Key Largo. The Key Largo mouse is a federally endangered species.

Florida Mouse
Podomys floridanus

Family: Rats and Mice (Muridae)

Size: L 7½-8¾" (19-22 cm); T 3-3½" (7.5-9 cm)

Weight: 1-1¾ oz. (28-50 g)

Description: Reddish brown back with lighter, redder sides. White chin, chest, belly, legs and feet. Long bicolored tail, brown above, white below, nearly naked and shorter than the length of head and body. Very large, round naked ears. Dark eyering. Each hind foot has 5 pads (tubercles) on the sole.

Origin/Age: native; 1-2 years

Compare: Cotton Mouse (pg. 71) is similar in color, but is much smaller, with a shorter tail and 6 pads on the sole of each hind foot. The Oldfield Mouse (pg. 59) is also smaller, but much lighter in color, with 6 pads on the sole of each hind foot.

Habitat: dry upland sandy soils with abundant oaks and pines

Home: nest, loose mass of plant material lined with animal hair, Spanish moss or other soft material, in an underground tunnel system, often using a Gopher Tortoise burrow

Food: omnivore; seeds, vegetation, fruit, nuts, insects, carrion

Sounds: inconsequential

Breeding: Jul-Dec mating; 22-23 days gestation

Young: 2-4 pups up to 2-3 times per year; born with eyes and ears closed

juvenile

Signs: evidence of a burrow next to or inside a Gopher Tortoise burrow, runways and surface tunnels radiating from the entrance of burrow, some entrances have dirt piled up; scat not seen

Activity: nocturnal; stays in the nest during heavy rain

Tracks: hind paw 1" (2.5 cm) long with 5 toes, forepaw ¾" (2 cm) long with 4 toes; 1 set of 4 tracks along trails leading to and from the burrow, showing a tail drag mark

Stan's Notes: Florida Mouse is found only in Florida (endemic). Its closest relatives are seen in central Mexico. Due to its limited range, the development of land, and dependence (commensal) on Gopher Tortoise burrows for shelter, it is listed as a species of special concern, with the possibility of being included on the state list as a threatened species. Populations have decreased significantly since the 1940s, with a rapid decrease occurring since the 1980s.

Also known as Florida Deer Mouse. Well known for its very large ears and apparently friendly nature. Also called Gopher Mouse due to its habit of using a Gopher Tortoise burrow for its home. Will dig inside the tortoise burrow and excavate side burrows for its own nest chamber. Nest is composed of a bed of dried leaves, Spanish moss or feathers.

When available, acorns are a major source of its food. Although it can climb, it dwells primarily on the ground (terrestrial). A prey species for predators such as owls, bobcats, foxes and coyotes.

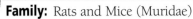

Key Rice Rat
Oryzomys argentatus

Family: Rats and Mice (Muridae)

Size: L 4¾-5" (12-13 cm); T 4-4½" (10-11 cm)

Weight: 1½-2½ oz. (43-71 g)

Description: Brown fur with silver-gray sides and off-white to gray below. Short wide snout. Small round ears. Dark eyes. Scaly tail, shorter than the length of the body and head combined.

Origin/Age: native; 1-2 years

Compare: Nearly identical to the Marsh Rice Rat (pg. 83), but has silver-gray sides. Much smaller than the Black Rat (pg. 87), which has a naked tail longer than its head and body. Smaller than the Hispid Cotton Rat (pg. 91), which has a stockier body and a more grizzled appearance.

Habitat: usually associated only with the marshes and wetlands of some of the Florida Keys

Home: shallow burrow above high water level or many round nests made of dry grasses, sedges or other plants, usually on slightly elevated tufts of grass, sometimes beneath logs and other debris above high water, occasionally uses an old bird nest

Food: omnivore; seeds, nuts, insects, carrion, birds, bird eggs, small mammals

Sounds: usually silent; makes inconsequential noises

Breeding: year-round mating; 20-25 days gestation; female can mate within hours of giving birth

Young: 2-4 (average 3) offspring up to 6 times per year; born naked with eyes closed, eyes open at about 5-6 days, weaned at 2 weeks

79

Signs: water trails along the surface at the water's edge, cut plants, cut plants on feeding platforms in shallow water

Activity: nocturnal; active year-round, can be active on cloudy days

Tracks: hind paw 1¼" (3 cm) long with a narrow heel and 5 toes, forepaw ¾" (2 cm) long with 4 well-spread toes; often follows the same paths over and over, making individual tracks difficult to distinguish

Stan's Notes: This rat is a great swimmer and climbs trees very well. The state of Florida and the federal government list it as an endangered species. Once thought to be a subspecies of Marsh Rice Rat (pg. 83). Many people still consider it to be a subspecies and do not recognize it as a full species. Also called Silver Rice Rat due to the silver color on its sides.

Lives in the salt marsh and in mangrove swamps. Found only in the Lower Keys (endemic) on Big Torch Key, Cudjoe Key, Howe Key, Johnston Key, Little Pine Key, Lower Sugarloaf Key, Middle Torch Key, Raccoon Key (largest population), Saddlebunch Keys, Summerland Key, Upper Sugarloaf Key and Water Key. Was first discovered in the marshes on Cudjoe Key.

Breeds year-round, but it seems to have a peak from September to October. An individual may build and use up to a dozen nests. Most are constructed on tufts of grass that are slightly elevated above the ground.

The territory is under 20 acres (8 ha). Territory size depends on how much fresh water is available, and fresh water is limited on the islands. Because of this, densities are very low and probably were never high.

Many of the islands have been colonized by the non-native Black Rat (pg. 87), which preys on the smaller, native rice rats. This may be the cause of its widespread decline in population.

Marsh Rice Rat
Oryzomys palustris

Family: Rats and Mice (Muridae)

Size: L 4½-5½" (11-14 cm); T 4-4½" (10-11 cm)

Weight: 1½-2½ oz. (43-71 g)

Description: Brown with grayish sides and off-white to gray below. Short wide snout. Small round ears. Dark eyes. Tail is scaly and not as long as the length of the body and head combined.

Origin/Age: native; 1-2 years

Compare: The Key Rice Rat (pg. 79) is slightly smaller and found only in the Florida Keys. Much smaller than Black Rat (pg. 87), which has a naked tail longer than its head and body. Smaller than the Hispid Cotton Rat (pg. 91), which looks more grizzled and has a stockier body.

Habitat: usually associated with marshes, wetlands, fresh water, saltwater and flooded fields

Home: shallow burrow above high water levels or round nests made of dried grasses, sedges or other plants, usually under logs and other debris above high water, occasionally uses an old bird nest

Food: omnivore; plants, rice, seeds, nuts, insects, birds, bird eggs, small mammals, carrion, snails, crabs

Sounds: usually silent; makes inconsequential noises

Breeding: year-round mating; 20-25 days gestation; female can mate within hours of giving birth

Young: 2-4 (average 3) offspring up to 6 times per year; born naked with eyes closed, eyes open at about 5-6 days, weaned at 2 weeks

Signs: water trails along the surface at the water's edge, cut plants, cut plants on feeding platforms in shallow water

Activity: nocturnal; active year-round, can be active on cloudy days

Tracks: hind paw 1" (2.5 cm) long with a narrow heel and 5 toes, forepaw ½" (1 cm) long with 4 well-spread toes; often follows the same paths over and over, making individual tracks difficult to distinguish

Stan's Notes: This is a small, semiaquatic native rat with a good disposition and habits. Not usually aggressive and does not enter homes or barns, staying mainly in wetlands where it feeds on green plants. Occurs from the eastern edge of Texas to throughout Florida, up the East coast to Maryland and west to the southern tip of Illinois.

Swims underwater, searching for the tender parts of underwater plants. Also eats aquatic insects, snails and tiny crabs. Consumes equal amounts of plant and animal matter, the diet changing with the season and the season's abundance of food. Apparently has an affinity for cultivated rice, which accounts for its common name.

This animal is so small and occurs in such low density, it usually never causes damage to crops or wetland plants and therefore goes unnoticed. Constructs feeding platforms in wetlands with woven grasses and other vegetation. Will bring food back to the platform to eat.

Strictly nocturnal. A similar population found on Sanibel Island, known as Sanibel Island Rice Rat (*O. p. sanibeli*) (not shown), is considered a subspecies of Marsh Rice Rat.

Signs: holes chewed in barn walls or doors, well-worn paths along walls or that lead in and out of chewed holes, smell of urine near the nest site; large, hard, cylindrical, dark brown-to-black droppings deposited along trails

Activity: nocturnal; active year-round, can be active on cloudy days

Tracks: hind paw 1⅜" (3.5 cm) long with a narrow heel and 5 toes, forepaw 1" (2.5 cm) long with 4 well-spread toes; often follows the same paths over and over, making individual tracks difficult to distinguish

Stan's Notes: The Black Rat, a non-native mammal from Asia, is the infamous species that carried bubonic plague. It is by far the most abundant of introduced rats in the state. Common in both rural and urban areas of Florida, on farms and ranches, as well as in back alleys of the largest cities. A climber, seen in barn rafters and running on power lines. Also called House Rat and Roof Rat because it is often seen in homes and on rooftops. Known as Ship Rat since it was found on large sailing ships.

Often makes its nest in the thatch of palm trees. Seen scampering up and down palm tree trunks at night. Comes out at night to feed on palm fruit and can be heard moving about in the trees.

There are many subspecies of Black Rat. Only a few of these are actually black, making it hard to differentiate from Norway Rat (pg. 95). One way to tell them apart is to note the tail length. The Black Rat has a longer tail than the length of its head and body combined; Norway Rat has a shorter tail.

Believed to have been first introduced to America in 1609 by the early settlers at Jamestown. It has since spread across the country on its own. Was once much more common in the United States. With the introduction of the Norway Rat, Black Rat numbers have declined.

Signs: nests made with plant material aboveground and below, well-worn runways in grass

Activity: nocturnal, crepuscular; active year-round, can be active on cloudy days

Tracks: hind paw 1½" (4 cm) long with a narrow heel and 5 toes, forepaw 1" (2.5 cm) long with 4 well-spread toes; often follows the same paths over and over, making individual tracks difficult to distinguish when it has been walking

Stan's Notes: Cotton rats have a stocky body, short round snout, coarse grizzled fur and pleasant disposition. The Hispid is one of the largest of the four cotton rat species in the United States and is the only one that occurs in Florida.

Cotton rats are active year-round and can be active at any time of day, depending on weather. During rainy years they reproduce much more, with a marked decrease in reproduction during drought years.

Nests are either in chambers underground or aboveground in dense clumps of grass. Similar to harvest mice, the aboveground nests are ball-shaped masses of dried plant material.

Main food is green grass and when available, seeds. This rat will also feed on insects and the eggs of ground-nesting birds.

Marks territories with scents indicating sex, dominance and sexually readiness. Also uses visual signals, such as body postures, to communicate between individuals.

Can breed up to 5 times a year in the wild and up to 10 times a year in captivity. Females often breed shortly after giving birth. Becomes sexually mature in 40 days. Young rats look different from their parents until they reach 6 months. Only the females care for the young.

The common name "Hispid," originating from Latin, refers to its dark, grizzled, stiff hairs and accurately describes the appearance of this tame and timid critter. An important source of food for many predators such as bobcats, coyotes, hawks, eagles, falcons and just about anything that can catch them.

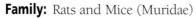

Norway Rat
Rattus norvegicus

Family: Rats and Mice (Muridae)

Size: L 8-10" (20-25 cm); T 5-8" (13-20 cm)

Weight: ½-1 lb. (.2-.5 kg)

Description: Brown to grayish brown above and gray below. Long narrow snout. Large round ears. Dark eyes. Scaly tail, shorter than the body length.

Origin/Age: non-native; 2-4 years

Compare: Larger than all mice, shrews and voles. The Black Rat (pg. 87) has a longer tail than its head and body combined. Eastern Woodrat (pg. 99) has a well-furred tail. The Hispid Cotton Rat (pg. 91) is smaller and appears more grizzled. Look for large ears and a long naked tail that is shorter than the head and body length to help identify the Norway Rat.

Habitat: cities, dumps, homes, farms

Home: network of tunnels, 2-3" (5-7.5 cm) wide and up to 6' (1.8 m) long, with inner chambers for sleeping and feeding, often has several escape exits and dead-end tunnels for hiding

Food: omnivore; seeds, nuts, insects, carrion, birds, bird eggs, small mammals

Sounds: high-pitched squeaks if squabbling with other rats; scratching, gnawing or scampering at night

Breeding: year-round mating; 20-25 days gestation; female can mate within hours of giving birth

Young: 2-9 (average 6) offspring up to 10 times per year; born naked with eyes closed, eyes open at about 2 weeks, weaned at 3-4 weeks

Signs: holes chewed in barn walls or doors, well-worn paths along walls or that lead in and out of chewed holes, smell of urine near the nest site; large, hard, cylindrical, dark brown-to-black droppings deposited along trails

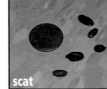
scat

Activity: nocturnal; active year-round, can be active on cloudy days

Tracks: hind paw 1½" (4 cm) long with a narrow heel and 5 toes, forepaw 1" (2.5 cm) long with 4 well-spread toes; often follows the same paths over and over, making individual tracks difficult to distinguish

Stan's Notes: A rat of cities large and small as well as rural areas, including farms. This animal has greatly benefited from its association with people. It has adapted well to city environments, feeding on discarded food and carrion. In farm settings, it eats stored food such as grain.

Also known as Common Rat, Brown Rat, Water Rat or Sewer Rat. A good swimmer and climber. Tolerates cold temperatures well. Excavates by loosening dirt with its front feet, pushes dirt under its belly, then turns and pushes dirt out with its head and front feet. Will chew through roots when they are in the way. A true omnivore, it sometimes acts like a predator, killing chickens and other small farm animals. Can be aggressive if backed into a corner or during a run-in with the family dog. Able to reproduce quickly, especially when food is abundant.

Has a very small territory with a high population density. Will migrate upon occasion. Large numbers have been seen leaving an area, presumably in response to overcrowding and a dwindling food supply.

Despite its common name, the Norway Rat is thought to originate from central Asia. It was introduced to different parts of the world via trading ships in the 1600-1700s and is believed to have been brought to North America in ships that transported grain in the eighteenth century. The name "Norway" actually comes from the fact this species was scientifically described in Norway.

This is the same species as the white rats used in lab experiments. A carrier of disease and fleas and should be exterminated when possible. However, it is difficult to trap and exterminate because its home usually has several escape exits. Due to intense human pressure for eradication (artificial selection), it has now become resistant to many types of rat poisons.

Eastern Woodrat
Neotoma floridana

EASTERN KEY LARGO

Family: Rats and Mice (Muridae)

Size: L 7¼-11½" (18.5-29 cm); T 6-7" (15-18 cm)

Weight: 10-16 oz. (284-454 g)

Description: A large mouse-like gray rat. Brown flanks. Gray-to-white (or creamy white) chin, chest and belly. Long pointed snout. Large round ears and large dark eyes. Tail much shorter than body, sharply bicolored, dark above, well furred, lacks a tufted tip. Long black and white whiskers. White feet.

Origin/Age: native; 1-3 years

Compare: The Black Rat (pg. 87) has a very long naked tail and lacks a white chin. Norway Rat (pg. 95) is smaller and has a much shorter tail.

Habitat: wide variety of habitats such as rocky areas, wetlands, scrublands, brushlands and forests

Home: small debris pile or very large nest of many sticks, branches, bones and more (midden), chamber lined with dry vegetation, by a large tree, log or in an abandoned building, with many entrances, can be used by many individual rats over time

Food: herbivore; wide variety of green plants, grasses, fruits, seeds, berries, fungi, very few insects

Sounds: thumping or drumming created by the hind feet, very vocal with much squabbling during flights

Breeding: year-round mating; 25-35 days gestation

Young: 1-5 (average 3) offspring up to 2-3 times per year; born naked with eyes closed, opening at 15 days, weaned at 62-72 days, doesn't become sexually mature until 5-6 months

Key Largo

Signs: large dome-shaped stick house (midden), reminiscent of a brush pile, containing hundreds of sticks, bark, bones and whatever else the animal is able to carry, well-worn trails leading out and away from the midden in many directions, piles of scat outside the midden; pellet-shaped waste

Activity: nocturnal; active year-round, can be active on cloudy days

Tracks: hind paw 1¾" (4.5 cm) long with a narrow heel and 5 toes, forepaw 1¼" (3 cm) long with 4 well-spread toes; frequently follows the same paths over and over, making individual tracks difficult to distinguish when it has been hopping

Stan's Notes: Also called Florida Woodrat. By far the most wide ranging of woodrats. Several species occur in the western half of the country, but this is the only one in the eastern United States. From central Florida, range extends up the East coast to North Carolina, west to Kansas and south to eastern Texas.

Often called Pack Rat due to its habit of collecting sticks, bark, bones and even shiny metal or mineral objects that it stores in and around its den, called a midden. Digs a network of tunnels beneath the midden, especially when there is a limited supply of materials and the midden is small. Builds its nest at the base of a large tree, next to a fallen log or inside an abandoned building.

A solitary animal that is found with others only during mating season and when young are with their mothers. Very aggressive toward one another during the non-breeding season. Fights are common and result in torn ears and damaged tails. Sometimes individuals also have scars on their bodies.

Lodges shed water well, keeping the interior dry and temperate. Does not defecate or urinate in its home, but has a separate toilet outside–evident by piles of pellet-shaped droppings. Normally nocturnal, but sometimes can be seen outside on a cloudy day.

Young are born with front teeth that permit them to grasp their mother's nipple and not let go. If the mother starts walking while nursing, the young will continue to clench and end up getting dragged behind her, bouncing along the ground on their backs.

The Key Largo Woodrat (*N. f. smalli*), a subspecies of the Eastern Woodrat, is found in a small area of northern Key Largo. The habits of the Key Largo are similar to those of Eastern Woodrat, but Key Largo lives in tropical hardwood hummocks and is listed as a federally endangered species.

Pine Vole
Microtus pinetorum

Family: Rats and Mice (Muridae)

Size: L 3¾-4½" (9.5-11 cm); T ½-1¼" (1-3 cm)

Weight: ¾-1¼ oz. (21-35 g)

Description: Overall chestnut brown fur with a glossy or shiny appearance and gray chest and belly. Short blunt snout. Tiny eyes. Small ears, but visible. Short bicolored tail, changing gradually from dark on top to light below.

Origin/Age: native; 1-2 years

Compare: Pine Vole has a bicolored tail that changes from dark above to light below gradually, unlike the tail of the Salt Marsh Vole (pg. 107), which has a sharp demarcation of color.

Habitat: deciduous forests with thick leaf litter and green ground cover, dense grass patches

Home: ball-shaped nest with a hollow center, made of dried grasses, usually underground in a network of tunnels; lives mainly below the surface; also maintains a series of surface tunnels

Food: herbivore; green plants in summer; roots, bulbs, seeds, berries and other fruit in winter

Sounds: inconsequential; chatters with up to 5 notes per call when threatened

Breeding: Feb-Oct mating; 20-24 days gestation

Young: 1-4 pups up to 4 times per year; born with eyes and ears closed, weaned at 17 days

Signs: well-worn runways and tunnels through thick vegetation

Activity: nocturnal, diurnal; active year-round, often active 24 hours, with several hours of rest followed by several hours of activity

Tracks: hind paw ⅝" (1.5 cm) long with 5 toes, forepaw ¼" (.6 cm) long with 4 toes; individual tracks are indistinguishable and create a single groove

Stan's Notes: Only two vole species (not including the muskrat) in Florida. Pine Vole is found in the northern half of the state and is much more common than Salt Marsh Vole (pg. 107), which occurs only in an isolated pocket of Florida.

A vole of deciduous forests that have a thick layer of decaying leaves and branches (duff). Sometimes called Woodland Vole. The common name "Pine" is somewhat of a misnomer since this species does not spend much time in coniferous habitats. The Latin species name *pinetorum* is also misleading because it refers to a pine habitat as well. Why these names have been applied is unknown. The genus name *Microtus* is Greek and refers to the small ears that are common to this genus.

The small body and ears, tiny eyes and large front claws suit it well for an underground (fossorial) life of digging. Digs out areas to cache food for consumption later.

The chestnut color, small size and unique tail help to identify the Pine Vole. Its bicolored tail is unlike that of all other vole species, gradually changing from dark above to light below.

Can be semi-colonial, with several families sharing a single nest chamber. Doesn't seem to have the "peak and crash" population cycles common to the other vole species. Owls, hawks, coyotes, foxes, minks and other predators all depend on these critters for a constant source of food.

ARE

Salt Marsh Vole
Microtus pennsylvanicus

Family: Rats and Mice (Muridae)

Size: L 4-5" (10-13 cm); T 1½-2½" (4-6 cm)

Weight: 1-2½ oz. (28-71 g)

Description: Overall dark gray with rusty red highlights and peppered with black. Gray chest and belly. Short round snout. Ears small, but visible. Tail is dark above, light below.

Origin/Age: native; 1-2 years

Compare: The Pine Vole (pg. 103) has a bicolored tail that changes gradually from dark above to light below, not like the sharply demarcated coloring of the Salt Marsh Vole's tail.

Habitat: wet grassy meadows and fields, moist woodland edges

Home: ball-shaped nest with a hollow center, made of dried grass, usually underneath a log or rock; lives above ground and underground; maintains a system of trails and tunnels

Food: herbivore; green grass, seeds, sedges

Sounds: inconsequential; chatters, grinds teeth and drums hind feet on the ground when threatened

Breeding: Apr-Nov mating, sometimes will mate in winter; 21 days gestation

Young: 3-10 pups (average 7) up to 15 times per year; weaned at about 2 weeks

Signs: well-worn runways in the grass; piles of freshly cut grass stacked up along runways

Activity: diurnal, nocturnal; active year-round, often active 24 hours a day with several hours of rest followed by several hours of activity, less active on nights with a full moon

scat

Tracks: hind paw ¾" (2 cm) long with 5 toes, forepaw ½" (1 cm) long with 4 toes; individual tracks are indistinguishable and create a single groove

Stan's Notes: Rare in Florida, with only an isolated population in the north central part of the state. Also called Meadow Vole. At times mistakenly called Meadow Mouse or Field Mouse, but this is not a mouse; does not enter homes like a mouse. Fares well in abandoned farmlands and most places that are moist and have thick grass, including fields.

While many other small mammals include insects in their diet, this is one of the few small animals that is strictly vegetarian.

Thought to have a social system in which females are territorial, with males moving freely in and around female territories. Tends to be solitary during the breeding season and gathers in non-breeding groups in winter. During periods of activity, it maintains runways, feeds, finds a mate and marks territory with urine and feces.

pups

The most prolific mammal on earth by far, with the female able to reproduce at 3 weeks. Female has a postpartum estrus, which allows her to mate almost immediately after giving birth.

This species is preyed upon by many larger mammals and birds when the population is abundant. Population cycles swing up and down every 2-5 years; unknown why or how this happens.

Round-tailed Muskrat
Neofiber alleni

Family: Rats and Mice (Muridae)

Size: L 6-10" (15-25 cm); T 5-7" (13-18 cm)

Weight: 6-12 oz. (170-340 g)

Description: Glossy dark brown fur, lighter on belly. Round, dark naked tail, covered with scales. Long tail, but not as long as the head and body combined. Small round ears, well hidden in dense fur. Tiny eyes. Large webbed hind feet. Long claws.

Origin/Age: native; 3-10 years

Compare: Round-tailed Muskrat has a longer, thinner tail than American Beaver (pg. 119), which is much larger and has a large flat tail. Much smaller than the Nutria (pg. 115), which has a large rounded head with a blunt snout.

Habitat: ponds, lakes, ditches, small rivers, streams

Home: small den, called a lodge, made of long grasses and other soft green (herbaceous) plant material, 1-2 underwater entrances, 1 chamber, not made with mud or woody plants

Food: herbivore; aquatic plants, maidencane grass and cattail shoots, roots and rhizomes

Sounds: inconsequential; squeaking, chewing sounds can be heard when feeding above water on feeding platform

Breeding: year-round mating; 25-30 days gestation

Young: 1-4 offspring 3-4 times per year; born naked with eyes closed, swims at about 2 weeks, weaned at about 3 weeks

Signs: well-worn trails through vegetation along a shore near a muskrat lodge, feeding platform made of floating plant material, 24" square (154.8 sq. cm), usually strewn with partially eaten plants; lodge made of fine grasses and other cut vegetation

Activity: nocturnal, crepuscular; active all year, doesn't hibernate, can be seen during the day

Tracks: hind paw 1½-2" (4-5 cm) long with 5 toes and a long heel, forepaw 1" (1.5 cm) with 5 toes spread evenly; hind paws fall near or onto fore prints (direct register) when walking, often obliterating the forepaw tracks; prints may show only 4 toes since the fifth toe is not well formed, often has a tail drag mark

Stan's Notes: A member of the Voles and Lemmings (Arvicolinae) subfamily, which is in the Rats and Mice (Muridae) family. Native only to Florida and Georgia. Not very common in Florida, seen in isolated pockets. Many parts of Florida have suitable habitat; however, no muskrats are found. Round-tailed is a close relative of Common Muskrat (not shown), which is a much more widespread species across the United States, but does not occur in Florida.

The musky odor (most evident in males during breeding season) emanating from two glands of its rat-like tail is the reason for the "Muskrat" common name. Some people say the common name is a derivation of the Algonquian Indian word *musquash*, which sounds somewhat like "muskrat."

Mostly aquatic, the muskrat is highly suited to living in water. It has a waterproof coat that protects it from water. Partially webbed hind feet and a fringe of hair along each toe help the muskrat to propel itself. The tail, which is round, also helps with forward motion and is used as a rudder. A good swimmer; swims backward and sideways with ease. Able to stay submerged for up to 15 minutes. Its mouth can close behind the front teeth only, allowing the animal to cut vegetation free while it is submerged. Surfaces to eat. May store some roots and tubers in mud below the water to consume during times of drought.

Lives with other muskrats in small groups, but there is no social structure; individuals act mainly on their own. Becomes sexually mature the first spring after its birth.

Lodges are built with fine grasses, with a flat platform inside. Two entrance/exit holes lead into the water below. A muskrat lodge is not like a beaver lodge, which is constructed with woody plant material and mud. While there is only one beaver lodge per lake or stream, there are often several muskrat lodges in a body of water. Does not defecate in the lodge, so the interior living space is kept remarkably clean.

Signs: well-worn trails through vegetation along wetlands, feeding platform constructed of floating plant material, 24" square (154.8 sq. cm), usually strewn with partially eaten cattails and other plants; nests made of cut vegetation; elongated scat found on feeding platforms or in shallow water

Activity: nocturnal; active year-round, does not hibernate

Tracks: hind paw 4½-5½" (10.5-14 cm) long with 5 toes (webbed) and a long heel, forepaw about half the size with 5 toes spread evenly; hind paws fall near fore prints when walking; hind prints may show only 4 toes since the fifth toe is not well formed and off to the side; may have a tail drag mark

Stan's Notes: A large aquatic rodent, nearly the size of a beaver. Introduced from South America in 1889 for its high-quality fur. Raised on ranches for its fur, it eventually escaped into the wild due to a variety of reasons. During the 1940s, the fur industry collapsed and many others were released into the wild.

Originally from semiaquatic habitats in southern Chile and farther south in Tierra del Fuego. One of the few mammals that can thrive in fresh water and saltwater. Today in Florida it has spread east to west starting on the East coast, moving as far west as the Texas panhandle. Reported in 22 states total, but occurs mainly in Gulf coast states.

An excellent swimmer, with only its ears, eyes and nostrils visible above the surface. Can dive and remained submerged for long periods of time to evade predators.

Competes with the smaller, local native muskrat species for the limited suitable habitats such as wetlands. Lives in a variety of homes, including burrows that it excavates itself or takes from others. Feeds, loafs, gives birth and escapes from predators on circular platforms built from vegetation, which are often mistaken for muskrat houses.

Breeds year-round and quickly overpopulates. Once established, it often eats most of the aquatic vegetation, causing extensive damage to wetlands. Eats all of the native vegetation that holds wetland soils together. A nocturnal animal, so usually only the damage is seen, not the culprit.

Considered an invasive species in the United States. Previously sold as a "natural" control for noxious weeds, this unfortunately also helped extend its range in nearly all states where it occurs. Efforts to control the population include government-sponsored programs to hunt and trap the animal. While South Americans enjoy its meat, efforts here to market it for consumption did not catch on with the public.

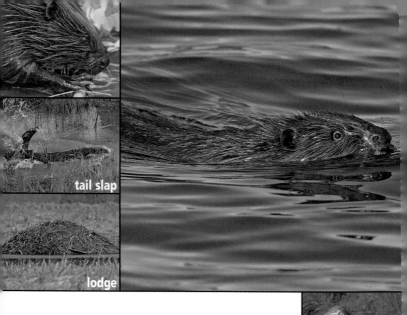

tail slap

lodge

scat

Signs: dam and lodge made from large woody branches can indicate current or former activity since structures remain well after the beaver has moved on or been killed, chewed tree trunks with large amounts of wood chips at the base of trees, flattened paths through vegetation leading to and from a lake; oval pellets, 1" (2.5 cm) long, containing sawdust-like material and bark, scat seldom on land

Activity: nocturnal, crepuscular; active year-round

Tracks: hind paw 5" (13 cm) long with 5 toes pointing forward and a long narrow heel, forepaw 3" (7.5 cm) with 5 splayed toes; wide tail drag mark often wipes out paw prints

Stan's Notes: This is the largest native rodent in Florida. Body is well suited for swimming. Valves close off the ears and nostrils when underwater, and a clear membrane covers the eyes. Can remain submerged up to 15 minutes. Webbed toes on hind feet help it swim as fast as 6 mph (10 km/h). Special lips seal the mouth yet leave the front incisors exposed, allowing it to carry branches in its mouth without water getting inside. At the lodge, it eats the soft bark of smaller branches the same way we eat corn on the cob. Doesn't eat the interior wood. Stores branches for later use by sticking them in mud on a lake or river bottom. A specialized claw on each hind foot is split like a comb and used for grooming.

Builds a dam to back up a large volume of water, creating a pond. Cuts trees at night by gnawing trunks. Uses larger branches to construct the dam and lodge. Cuts smaller branches and twigs of felled trees into 6-foot (1.8 m) sections. Dam repair is triggered by the sound of moving water, not by sight. Most repair activity takes place at night.

Given its genus name *Castor* for the pungent castor oil that it secretes from glands near the base of its tail. Uses castor to mark territories or boundaries called castor mounds. Castor oil from this gland is not the same castor oil from plants used in medicines.

Monogamous and mates for life. However, will take a new mate if partner is lost. Can live up to 20 years in captivity. Young remain with parents through their first winter. They help cut and store a winter food source and maintain the dam while parents raise another set of young. Young disperse at 2 years.

No other mammal except people changes the environment as much as beavers. Frogs, turtles and many bird species, including ducks, herons and egrets, benefit from the newly created habitat. Beavers have made a comeback in northern Florida after being killed off by excessive trapping and hunting. Their return has been on their own; no program was established for their reintroduction.

Capybara
Hydrochoerus hydrochaeris

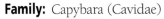

Family: Capybara (Cavidae)

Size: L 3-4' (.9-1.2 m); no tail

Weight: 40-100 lb. (18-45 kg)

Description: Tan to reddish brown or dark brown fur. Large round head with a short blunt snout. Small round ears and small dark eyes. Short stout legs with webbed feet. No tail.

Origin/Age: non-native; 10-15 years

Compare: Round-tailed Muskrat (pg. 111) is much smaller and has a long thin tail. Larger than the American Beaver (pg. 119), which has a large, flat black tail. Look for Capybara feeding out of the water on riverbanks and in wet fields.

Habitat: rivers, streams, ponds, lakes, ditches, wetlands, wherever water is present

Home: no den or permanent house; moves around in family units on land and in wetlands

Food: herbivore; soft bark, inner bark, aquatic plants, grasses, green leaves

Sounds: usually quiet

Breeding: May-Jun mating; 130-150 days gestation

Young: 2-4 young once per year; born with light tan fur, eyes open, weighing about 3-5 lb. (1.4-2.3 kg), able to follow mother within hours, eating on their own within a week, weaned at 16 weeks

123

Signs: short grazed grass along a riverbank; scat also found in the area

Activity: nocturnal, crepuscular; active year-round, can be seen during the day

Tracks: hind paw 5-6" (13-15 cm) long with 3 long round toes and a square heel, forepaw 3-5" (7.5-13 cm) with 4 short thick toes

Stan's Notes: This is the largest rodent in the world. An unusual non-native aquatic animal because of its webbed feet, which suit it well for its time in the water. Some estimate that 80-90 percent of its life is spent in water. An excellent swimmer, staying underwater for up to 5 minutes. Surfaces to catch a breath and look for danger, showing only its nostrils and eyes above water. Runs to water if threatened and completely submerges to escape danger.

One of the few animals without a tail. A calm and gentle animal, normally found in South America. People who kept it as a pet apparently introduced it into Florida. Many sightings have been reported over the past 20 years. Its closest living relatives are the Agouti, Chinchilla and Guinea Pig (none shown). Life span is 4-8 years.

This is a herbivore, grazing mainly on aquatic plants and grasses. Concentrates its diet on just a handful of plant species. Consumes 6-8 pounds (2.7-3.6 kg) of vegetation per day. Its common name *Kapiyva* from the Guarani language translates to "master of the grass," referring to its habit of grazing on grass along riverbanks. The genus and species names are Greek and mean "water hog."

A social animal, often in groups of up to 20 individuals. Groups are headed by a dominant male. Males are slightly smaller than females. Although adults usually weigh in at about 100 pounds (45 kg), some individuals have been recorded to be more than 200 pounds (90 kg). Fur of the adult Capybara is not dense and makes the animal vulnerable to sunburn. Wallows in mud and water to keep cool and to avoid the sun's harmful rays.

Females stray away to give birth to young and rejoin the group as soon as the young can walk and keep up. Young graze on grass within a week of birth.

large group

Signs: piles of dark brown-to-black scat under roosting sites

Activity: nocturnal; active only on warm dry nights, comes out approximately 30 minutes after sunset, feeds until full, roosts the rest of night, returns to daytime roost before sunrise

Tracks: none

Stan's Notes: A common bat of various habitats from scrublands to forest, cities to country. After wintering in Mexico and Central and South America, millions arrive during spring and take up residency in tunnels, caves, homes, beneath bridges and in other places providing a dark, comfortable roost. In Florida, this species inhabits old buildings and other structures and doesn't visit caves. Highly social, found roosting and flying in large groups.

Studies show that this bat feeds on many crop and forest pests and insects, making it a very beneficial animal to have around. It is estimated to eat 11-20 tons (10-18 mt) of insects annually.

A fast-flying bat, reaching speeds of 25 mph (40 km/h), with an erratic flight pattern, evident as it swoops and dives for beetles, mosquitoes and other flying insects. Often forages over rivers and lakes, beneath streetlights or wherever large groups of flying insects congregate. Emits a high-frequency (27-48 kHz) sound (inaudible to people) to locate prey and listens for returning echoes (echolocation). Most of these bats catch and eat one insect every three seconds, consuming $\frac{1}{10}$ ounce (3 g) per hour. During summer, when rapidly growing pups demand increasing amounts of milk, a lactating female can consume up to $\frac{7}{10}$ ounce (20 g) of insects every night, which is nearly equal to her own body weight.

A mother does not carry her pups during flight, but leaves them clinging to the roost until she returns. Holds pups to her chest under a wing to nurse. Recognizes young by their vocalizations.

Homeowners frequently discover bats when remodeling or adding onto their homes during winter months. Any unwanted bat found in homes should be professionally moved or removed to avoid hurting the animal.

Similar species on next page 129

There are 43 bat species in the United States, with 17 species in Florida. The order of bats, called Chiroptera, means "hand wing" and refers to the elongated fingers that all bats have with thin membranous skin stretched between. No other mammal besides the bat has the ability to fly.

All bats are nocturnal, with small eyes and large ears. They use high-frequency ultrasonic sounds (outside the hearing range of people) to avoid obstacles and find insect prey while in flight.

Bats live in all regions around the world except for polar regions. Several bat species roost in caves in Florida. These are usually females giving birth to pups. Species found in caves are the Little Brown Bat, Eastern Pipistrelle, Big Brown Bat, Gray Myotis and Southeastern Bat.

Little Brown Bat 1½"

Eastern Pipistrelle 2-2¼"

Evening Bat 1¾-2¼"

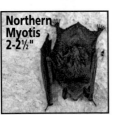
Northern Myotis 2-2½"

Big Brown Bat 2-3"

Silver-haired Bat 2-3"

Eastern Red Bat
2-3"

Indiana Bat
1¾-3½"

Hoary Bat
2-4"

Gray Myotis
3-3¼"

Little Mastiff Bat 3-3¼"

Wagner's Bonneted Bat 3-4"

Southeastern Bat 3¼-3⅞"

Rafinesque's Big-eared Bat 3⅞-4¼"

Northern Yellow Bat 4-4½"

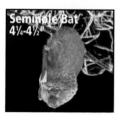
Seminole Bat 4¼-4½"

cheek pouch

burrow entrance

Signs: piles of cracked seeds and acorns and other food on a log or large rock; oblong dark brown pellets, ⅛" (.3 cm) long, often not seen and not key in identifying this species

Activity: diurnal; peak activity in the morning and evening, no activity on cold, windy or rainy days

Tracks: hind paw 1¼-1½" (3-4 cm) long with 5 toes, forepaw with 4 toes is about half the size of hind paw; 1 set of 4 tracks; hind paws fall in front of fore prints; tracks rarely seen since it lives in a dry rocky habitat

Stan's Notes: Very limited range, but uncommon only in Florida. Range extends from Minnesota to New England and south to the Gulf coast. The Latin genus name *Tamias* means "storer" and refers to its habit of storing large amounts of food in preparation for winter.

Known for loud vocalizations, which almost always are accompanied by a dramatic flick of the tail. Both the male and female vocalize. Usually sounds off while on a favorite perch, where it can survey its territory.

Doesn't cause damage to gardens, as some may think. Its burrows actually help to aerate the ground. Consumes great quantities of seeds that would otherwise germinate in lawns and gardens.

Chipmunks are delightful to watch and many people like to feed them. Can be very tame and tolerant of people. Usually solitary and very commonly seen around human dwellings. Maintains a small territory around the main burrow and will defend it from other "chippies." Has short, dead-end burrows for quick escapes.

Will eat just about anything from plants to animals. Comfortable climbing trees to gather seeds, buds and flowers for food. Can transport large amounts of food, usually seeds, in cheek pouches. Stores large quantities of seeds, nuts and dried berries in an underground cavity connected to its living chambers. Will eat from its cache when it cannot get outside to due weather and in winter.

A light hibernator, waking every 2-3 weeks to eat its stored food. Can occasionally be seen aboveground during warm spells in winter. Common to see it in February, although it usually goes back to sleep until March, when mating season begins.

Breeding season begins a few weeks after it emerges from hibernation, and lasts only a few weeks. Male emerges before female. Female can have two litters per season, but this is not common. Male takes no part in raising young.

Southern Flying Squirrel
Glaucomys volans

Family: Squirrels (Sciuridae)

Size: L 5-7" (13-18 cm); T 3-5" (7.5-13 cm)

Weight: 1½-2½ oz. (43-71 g)

Description: Light brown-to-gray fur above. White underside. Wide flat tail, gray above and white below. Large, bulging dark eyes. Loose fold of skin between the front and hind legs.

Origin/Age: native; 2-5 years

Compare: The flying squirrel is the only nocturnal squirrel. Can be identified by the wide flat tail and large bulging eyes.

Habitat: large trees, along rivers and streams, woodlands, urban and suburban yards and parks, prefers hummocks where Spanish moss is abundant

Home: nest lined with soft plant material, usually in an old woodpecker hole, sometimes in a nest box or an attic in homes and outbuildings, may build a small round nest of leaves on a tree branch; nest is similar to that of the Eastern Gray Squirrel (pg. 141), only smaller

Food: omnivore; seeds, nuts, carrion, baby mice, baby birds, bird eggs, lichens, mushrooms, fungi

Sounds: faint bird-like calls during the night, young give high-pitched squeaks

Breeding: spring mating; 40 days gestation

Young: 2-6 (average 3) offspring, 2 litters per year

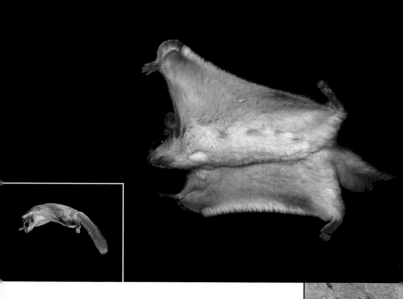

Signs: food has mysteriously disappeared from bird feeders overnight

Activity: nocturnal; active year-round, sometimes enters torpor during the very coldest parts of winter

scat

Tracks: hind paw 1" (2.5 cm) long with 5 toes, forepaw ½" (1 cm) long with 4 toes; 1 set of 4 tracks; large landing mark (sitzmark) followed by bounding tracks, with hind paws falling in front of front prints; tracks lead to the base of a tree

138

Stan's Notes: The flying squirrel is the only nocturnal member of the Squirrels family in Florida. Its large bulging eyes enable it to see well at night. Common name "Flying" is a misnomer because this animal does not have the capability to fly, only the ability to glide. In part, this is due to a large flap of skin (patagium) that is attached to its front and hind legs and to the sides of its body.

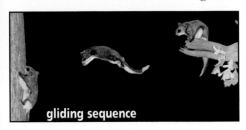

gliding sequence

To glide, the flying squirrel will climb to the top of a tree and launch itself forward, extending all four legs outward and stretching the patagium to make a flat, wing-like airfoil. Its flat tail adds some additional lift and acts like a rudder to help maneuver objects while gliding. Most glides are as long as 20-50 feet (6.1-15 m) and terminate at the trunk of another tree. To create an air brake for a soft landing, the squirrel will quickly lift its head and tuck its tail between its hind legs. After landing, it will scamper to the opposite side of the tree trunk, presumably to avoid any flying predators that may be following.

The flying squirrel is the most carnivorous of the tree squirrels, finding, killing and eating small mice, dead flesh (carrion) and even baby birds and bird eggs. It is a gregarious animal, with many individuals living together in a nest.

Young are born helpless with eyes closed. Weaned at 5-7 weeks, they may stay with their mother through their first winter. Most flying squirrels live only 2-5 years, but some have lived as long as 10 years in captivity.

Eastern Gray Squirrel
Sciurus carolinensis

Family: Squirrels (Sciuridae)

Size: L 8-9" (20-23 cm); T 8-9" (20-23 cm)

Weight: 12-24 oz. (340-680 g)

Description: Overall gray or light brown fur with a white chest and belly. Large, bushy gray tail with silver-tipped hairs. Black morph is overall black with a reddish brown shine. Tail may also be reddish brown.

Origin/Age: native; 2-5 years

Compare: Smaller than the Fox Squirrel (pg. 149), which has a rusty tail and dark forehead. The Southern Flying Squirrel (pg. 137) is smaller, with large dark eyes and a flat tail.

Habitat: woodlands, suburban and urban yards, parks, mangrove forests, tropical hummocks

Home: leaf nest (drey) in summer, hollow with a single entrance hole and lined with soft plant material, nest is in a tree cavity or old woodpecker hole in winter; male and female live in separate nests in summer, but together in winter

Food: omnivore; nuts, seeds, birdseed, fruit, corn, leaf buds, flowers, mushrooms, inner tree bark, baby birds, bird eggs, small mammals, insects, carrion

Sounds: repeats hoarse, wheezy calls when upset, chatters an alarm call to warn of predators such as cats

Breeding: Jan-Feb mating; 40-45 days gestation

Young: 2-6 offspring once (sometimes twice) per year; born naked with eyes closed, eyes open at about 5 weeks, weaned at about 8-9 weeks, mother pushes young away shortly after weaning

albino

black morph

Signs: acorns and other large nuts split in half with the nutmeat missing, gnaw marks on tree branches stripped of bark, trees that lack new branches with green leaves in early summer

scat

Activity: diurnal; active year-round, feeds late in morning and throughout the day, often rests a couple hours in the afternoon, may stay in nest for several days during very cold or hot periods

Tracks: hind paw 2¼" (5.5 cm) long with 5 toes, forepaw 1" (2.5 cm) long with 4 toes; 1 set of 4 tracks; forepaws fall side by side and behind hind prints

Stan's Notes: Common across Florida in nearly any place that has trees, especially oaks, which provide acorns. Pockets of black morph squirrels occur throughout the state. The black morph is born black and remains black. The albino morph, an entirely white squirrel with pink eyes, is more rare and does not live as long as the black morph.

Spends most of its life in trees, going to the ground only to feed on fallen nuts and seeds. Buries large amounts of nuts, most only ¼ inch (.6 cm) underground. Studies show about 85 percent of these nuts are recovered. Nuts buried by scientists were recovered at a similar rate, indicating that squirrels find buried food by smell, not memory. Many squirrels "migrate" in years with poor nut crops, moving to find a new home range with adequate food.

During the mating season, males will chase the females. Mating chases are long, with much jumping, bounding and biting.

Leaf nests (dreys) are located away from the main trunk of a tree and are constructed to shed water. A squirrel can have up to seven dreys, which are sometimes used as emergency nests. Usually born in a cavity nest, babies may be moved to a drey when the mother feels threatened. Mothers raise their young alone and move them from nest to nest, perhaps to avoid flea infestations. Studies show that 80 percent die in their first year due to predation by animals that eat squirrels such as coyotes, foxes and hawks.

leaf nest

Considered a nuisance by many because it eats birdseed. Eats a variety of foods, however, including some mushrooms that are poisonous to people. Famous for its ability to access nearly any bird feeder, spending hours, days or weeks devising a way to get the food. An industry has flourished around squirrel-proof feeders.

Red-bellied Squirrel
Sciurus aureogaster

Family: Squirrels (Sciuridae)

Size: L 9-10½" (23-27 cm); T 9-10" (23-25 cm)

Weight: 12-16 oz. (340-454 g)

Description: Highly variable in color. Overall gray to silver. Often has a red patch on nape of neck. Red ears, face and top of head. Rust red belly and inside of legs, often extending up onto sides. Large, bushy gray tail with red highlights. Often has black feet and lower legs. Some individuals are entirely black (melanistic).

Origin/Age: non-native; 2-5 years

Compare: The Eastern Gray Squirrel (pg. 141) lacks red on its nape, belly and tail. Smaller than the Fox Squirrel (pg. 149), which has a rusty orange tail.

Habitat: Elliott Key only

Home: leaf nest (drey) in summer, hollow with a single entrance hole and lined with soft plant material, also in natural cavities in trees; male and female live separately in summer, together in winter

Food: omnivore; nuts, seeds, leaf buds, flowers, insects, carrion, fruit and leaves of the sea grape, papaya, gumbo-limbo, coconut and palm

Sounds: usually silent; repeats hoarse, wheezy calls many times if upset or threatened, chatters an alarm call to warn of predators such as house cats

Breeding: year-round mating; 40-45 days gestation

Young: 1-2 offspring once (sometimes twice) per year; born naked with eyes closed, eyes open at about 4-5 weeks, weaned at about 7-8 weeks

145

black morph

Signs: acorns and other large nuts split in half with the nutmeat missing, gnaw marks on tree branches stripped of bark, leaf nests in trees

Activity: diurnal; active year-round, feeds late in morning and throughout the day, often rests a couple hours in the afternoon, may stay in nest for several days during very cold or hot periods

Tracks: hind paw 2½-3" (6-7.5 cm) long with 5 toes, forepaw 1" (2.5 cm) long with 4 toes; 1 set of 4 tracks; forepaws fall side by side and behind hind prints

Stan's Notes: A non-native species introduced to Elliott Key in 1938. Has since established itself, breeding and reproducing. No other squirrel species occurs on the island. While the Eastern Gray Squirrel (pg. 141) is the native squirrel on Key Largo and the Florida mainland, Red-bellied Squirrel is native to southern Mexico and Guatemala. Also known by another common name that indicates its origin–Mexican Gray Squirrel.

Not as easily seen as Eastern Gray Squirrels; apparently the Red-bellied island population avoids humans. In the normal range it can be very common and friendly, often taking food directly from the hands of people.

Some have estimated that up to half the population of Red-bellied Squirrels are black morphs (melanistic). Black morphs are born black and stay black their entire life. A gray Red-bellied Squirrel is often seen with a black morph, which can be a sibling or other family member.

Leaf nests (dreys) are constructed in tall trees, close to the main trunk. Also uses natural cavities in trees. Studies indicate most nests are located in the largest oak trees in forests.

During the breeding season, males chase females. Mating chases are long, with much jumping, bounding and biting, ending in mating. Mothers raise their young alone and move them from nest to nest, perhaps to avoid flea infestations. The record for the longest living captive Red-bellied Squirrel is 11½ years.

Eastern Sherman's
Big Cypress
black morph   white morph

Signs: large debris pile of split nutshells, whole corncobs and husks strewn about underneath the feeding perch

Activity: diurnal; active year-round, usually begins feeding late in the morning, several hours after sunrise, often active during the middle of the day

Tracks: hind paw 2¾-3" (7-7.5 cm) long with 5 toes, forepaw 1½" (4 cm) long with 4 toes; 1 set of 4 tracks; forepaws fall side by side and behind hind prints

Stan's Notes: Fox Squirrels in Florida have at least some black, hence the species name *niger*. "Fox" refers to the fox-like fluffy tail.

The largest tree squirrel, with 10 subspecies in the United States. Nearly all parts of Florida except the Keys have Fox Squirrels. All are subspecies of the more widespread Eastern Fox Squirrel (*S. niger*). Three subspecies live in Florida. Sherman's Fox Squirrel, seen in the peninsula, is the most widespread. Big Cypress Fox Squirrel, also called Mangrove Fox Squirrel, is the smallest, rarest and lives in southwestern Florida in mangrove swamps. Carolina Fox Squirrel is the largest, looks similar to Eastern Fox Squirrel and occurs in the panhandle. Black morphs are common across the state; white morphs are rare. Sherman's and Big Cypress are protected species. No Fox Squirrels may be hunted in Florida.

Sometimes takes food to its favorite spot to eat. The home range is 10 times larger than that of the Eastern Gray Squirrel (pg. 141)– up to 50 acres (20 ha)–so only several Fox Squirrels are found in any given area. Found in a variety of forested habitats, mainly in open pine woodlands, with oak and cypress trees along rivers and streams. In parks and golf courses it is sometimes fed by people.

leaf nest

Seen in dry pine-oak woods in central Florida. In southern Florida it is found in slash pine, cypress and cabbage palms.

The tannin in the acorns it eats is highly toxic to tapeworms and roundworms; thus, Fox Squirrels rarely host these parasites. Other than acorns, pine seeds are the favorite food.

Several males "chase" one female prior to mating, following her throughout the day. Females will mate with more than one male. Mating occurs in late winter and again in midsummer. Females begin to breed at 1 year and produce only a single litter per year.

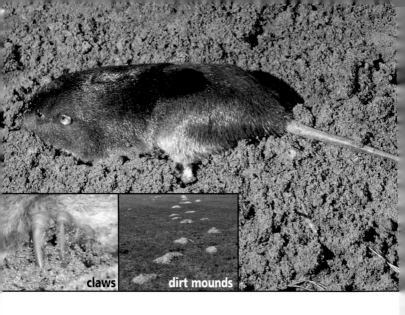

claws

dirt mounds

Signs: mounds of excess dirt as wide as 24" (61 cm) resulting from tunneling; ridges of dirt pushed up from tunneling; opening to tunnel system only rarely seen (would require digging into a dirt mound)

Activity: diurnal, nocturnal; active year-round, alternates several hours of activity with several hours of sleep

Tracks: forepaw 1-1½" (2.5-4 cm) long, hind paw ¾" (2 cm), both with well-defined claw marks; spends almost all of its time in its underground tunnel system, so tracks are rarely seen

Stan's Notes: There are 35 gopher species, all unique to North America. Southeastern Pocket Gopher is the only one that occurs in Florida.

Specialized fur-lined cheek pouches or "pockets" give the pocket gopher its common name. Able to stuff large amounts of food or nesting material in its pouches, which extend from its cheeks to front shoulders. Cleans the pouches by turning them inside out.

Digs with its powerful front legs and long sharp claws, preferring loose sandy soils. Specialized lips close behind its large incisor teeth, keeping dirt out of the mouth while it digs. Incisor teeth are coated with enamel and grow throughout its life. Must gnaw on hard objects to keep its teeth sharp and prevent them from growing too large and rendering them useless. Sensitive hairs and bristles (vibrissae) on the wrists and tip of tail help it feel its way through tunnels. A narrow pelvis enables it to turn around while in tunnels. Its fur can lay forward or backward and allows the animal to back up without slowing down. Has a good sense of smell, but poor hearing and eyesight. Holds its eyes tightly closed when tunneling to keep out sand. Able to tolerate low levels of oxygen and high levels of carbon dioxide which are a result of living in tunnels that are sealed off from the outside air.

Lives entirely underground. Feeds on roots and bulbs of different plant species, depending upon the season and availability, and stores some food in underground chambers. Has been known to pull entire plants underground by the roots. Solitary except to mate, with only one animal living in a set of tunnels and mounds.

Has adapted well to human activity, often taking up residence in open grassy yards. This animal is very beneficial to the land since its digging aerates the soil, which allows for better drainage and nutrient mixing. However, it can be destructive to gardens and fields because it eats many of the plants.

Squirrel Monkey
Saimiri sciureus

Family: Old World Monkeys (Cebidae)

Size: L 10-12" (25-30 cm); T 12-17" (30-43 cm)

Weight: 1½-2⅓ lb. (.7-1 kg)

Description: A small primate with gray and orange-to-tan fur, grizzled with black. Orange legs. White mask, chest and belly. Black around mouth and nose. White fur on ears. Long fingers and toes. Long, furry semiprehensile tail.

Origin/Age: non-native; 5-15 years

Compare: Smaller than Rhesus Monkey (pg. 161), which has a pink face and lacks black markings on its muzzle.

Habitat: woodlands

Home: leaf nest in trees, makes a new nest each night in the larger limbs of a tree

Food: omnivore; mainly fruit and insects it gathers from trees; also eats nuts, seeds, leaf buds, flowers, baby birds, bird eggs, lizards and small mammals

Sounds: many calls including loud warning calls when predators are near, softer interpersonal communications among family members

Breeding: Sep-Nov mating; 160-170 days gestation

Young: 1 offspring once per year; born furred, with eyes open, but helpless; weaned at 4 months, but not fully weaned until 1½ years of age

Signs: half-eaten fruit on the ground beneath food trees, calling and other sounds of activity coming from the trees

Activity: diurnal; active year-round, feeds late in morning and throughout the day, often rests a couple hours in the afternoon

Tracks: none (this monkey does not come down from trees); foot 2" (5 cm) long with 5 toes, hand 1½" (4 cm) long with 5 fingers

Stan's Notes: This species is the smallest of the monkeys. Can be found in the wild in a few areas of the state such as Dade County, the city of Naples and Polk County near Lake Wales. Squirrel monkeys come from the tropical forests of the Andes, Colombia, northern Peru and Brazil. There are five species, but only one occurs in Florida.

All monkeys in Florida are the result of introductions of escaped pets. Once imported to the United States for medical research and the pet trade, but federal regulations in 1975 stopped the importation of primates as pets.

Like the other primates, this is a social animal that travels and lives in groups known as troops. In its native range, as many as 300 individuals make up a troop. There is a strict hierarchy in troops, with females forming the central core. Dominant females reassert their dominance over younger females on a regular basis.

Lives in trees (arboreal) and rarely, if ever, comes down to the ground. Due to its small size, it is prey for most ground-dwelling predators along with some avian predators such as eagles. Does not seem to notice people, but tends to avoid them.

Squirrel monkeys spend most of their days gathering fruit and insects, taking naps and grooming each other. Youngsters play with other young. When climbing or traveling through trees, uses its semiprehensile tail as a balancing pole, but does not use it to aid climbing. Often curls its tail over a shoulder when at rest.

Females become sexually mature at 3 years of age; males mature at 5 years. Only the males have large canine teeth. Lives up to 15 years in the wild and over 20 years in captivity.

Of all primates, squirrel monkeys have the largest brains in proportion to their bodies. They are extremely intelligent, with a brain mass to body mass ratio of 1:17. This is more than twice as much as the human brain mass to body mass ratio of 1:40.

mother and young

Signs: half-eaten fruit on the ground beneath food trees, calling and other sounds of activity coming from the trees

Activity: diurnal; active year-round, feeds late in morning and throughout the day, often rests a couple hours in the afternoon

Tracks: foot 4" (10 cm) long with 5 toes, hand 3" (7.5 cm) long with 5 fingers; walks on 2 feet only; pair of tracks is similar to a pair of human footprints, bowlegged with toes pointing outward

Stan's Notes: An introduced species, with two colonies in Florida. One is on an island in the Lower Keys and is maintained by a pharmaceutical company that provides animals for research. The other is at Silver Springs near Ocala. Apparently was introduced when several monkeys were released on an island as part of a greater exhibit of animals in the late 1930s. The monkeys swam away and established themselves in the wild, where they've been ever since. Originally from Afghanistan and the Indochina region. In its native range, population is decreased due to human conflict. Still, it is the most widespread primate, second only to people.

Can be very aggressive and unfriendly. Males can be particularly aggressive and are known to attack people who appear to be staring. Presumably staring is a threatening behavior to monkeys.

Lives in large groups, known as troops, of up to several hundred. There is a dominant hierarchy within the group in both sexes, especially among males, with many fights breaking out. Females don't seem to fight. Once the group gets too large it is broken off into smaller groups, headed by other dominate members. Young males always leave their troops to find outside troops.

Troops are not very territorial. Within territories, groups often overlap. When a weaker group meets a stronger, more dominant group, the weaker one usually leaves to avoid conflict.

A good swimmer. Spends much time on the ground. Feeds on the ground and in trees. Hoards food temporarily in its cheek pouches.

Very active and can be loud. Highly promiscuous. Females solicit copulation with multiple males. Males mate with females many times before conception. In Florida, young are born in the spring.

Also called Rhesus Macaque. Used extensively in medical research and gave its name to the Rh factor (Rhesus factor) in blood types. During the U.S.-Soviet space race in the 1950-60s, Rhesus Monkeys were launched into space as the first living beings to go into space and return to earth alive.

Marsh Rabbit
Sylvilagus palustris

Family: Rabbits and Hares (Leporidae)

Size: L 13-17" (33-43 cm); T 1-1½" (2.5-4 cm)

Weight: 2-3½ lb. (.9-1.6 kg)

Description: Overall rusty brown or reddish brown short hair (pelage), grizzled with black. Paler on the sides to gray or white on belly. Small head compared with the body. Short, broad rounded ears, sparsely haired. Pale eye-ring. Short legs and small feet, all rusty red. Short puffy tail. Some individuals have a tiny amount of gray beneath. Large dark eyes.

Origin/Age: native; 1-3 years

Compare: Smaller than the Eastern Cottontail (pg. 169), which has larger, narrower ears and is overall gray with a rusty red nape.

Habitat: river bottoms, coastal marshes, mangroves, lowlands, wetlands, along streams, just about any other place with shallow standing water

Home: shallow nest, lined with soft plant material and fur, covered with dry grasses and leaves under a fallen log at the base of a tree

Food: herbivore; grass, other green plants, woody plants

Sounds: loud high-pitched scream or squeal when caught by a predator such as a fox, coyote or raptor, thumps feet on the ground

Breeding: Feb-Sep mating; 28-37 days gestation; starts to breed during the first year

Young: 2-4 offspring 3-5 times per year; born furred, with eyes and ears closed, opening within 4-5 days

Signs: runways in tall grass leading to and from wetlands, small woody twigs and branches near the ground are cleanly cut off and at an angle; pea-sized, round, dry, woody, light brown pellets

Activity: nocturnal, crepuscular; can also be seen during the day, often very active during February and March when males fight to breed with females

Tracks: hind paw 3½-4" (9-10 cm) long, forepaw ½" (1 cm) long, small and round, long nails; 1 set of 4 tracks; forepaws fall one in front of the other behind hind prints, front nails are often seen in tracks

Stan's Notes: An interesting rabbit species, very similar to Eastern Cottontail (pg. 169), but smaller, with shorter legs and ears and reddish fur. Found in most of Florida, usually not far from water. Lives in wet ditches, coastal marshes, swamps and along rivers and streams. Also seen on many of Florida's coastal islands. Truly a semiaquatic rabbit that will take to the water when pursued. Will swim to get where it wants to go such as islands. An excellent swimmer, often completely submerging except for its eyes and nostrils. Does not have special adaptations to help it swim. On land it often walks, unlike the other rabbits, which hop.

Reported to be the only rabbit species that can walk on its hind feet when foraging for food. Feeds on both terrestrial and aquatic green plants, and woody plants. Well known for creating surface tunnels (runways) through thick aquatic vegetation.

Its short legs make it less effective at eluding predators while running on land than other rabbit species. Will run a zigzag pattern when chased, often diving for cover when pursued.

During the day it creates a shallow depression in grass, called a form, to rest. Most active in early morning and at sunset. Moves about mainly at night, but can be seen regularly during the day.

Along the coast it lives in thickets, mangroves and barrier islands. A unique subspecies of the Marsh Rabbit, the Lower Keys Marsh Rabbit (*S. p. hefneri*) (not shown), occurs on only a few islands in the lower Florida Keys. The subspecies name *hefneri* refers to Hugh Hefner, who funded the research. The Lower Keys Marsh Rabbit is the only rabbit on the federal endangered species list. Loss of habitat, predation from domestic cats and mortality from highway traffic account for the decline of this subspecies. The Marsh Rabbit and Lower Keys Marsh Rabbit are the only rabbits found in the Florida Keys.

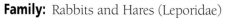

Eastern Cottontail
Sylvilagus floridanus

Family: Rabbits and Hares (Leporidae)

Size: L 14-18" (36-45 cm); T 1-2" (2.5-5 cm)

Weight: 2-4 lb. (.9-1.8 kg)

Description: Overall gray to light brown. Black-tipped hairs give it a grizzled appearance. Usually has a small white (rarely black) spot on forehead between the ears. Large pointed ears, rarely with a black outside edge. Distinctive rusty red nape. Brown tail with a white cotton-like underside.

Origin/Age: native; 1-3 years

Compare: Larger than Marsh Rabbit (pg. 165), which has shorter ears and a rusty red color. Much smaller than Black-tailed Jackrabbit (pg. 173).

Habitat: wide variety such as open fields, brush piles, rock piles, along rivers and streams, woodlands, thickets

Home: shallow nest, lined with soft plant material and fur, covered with dry grasses and leaves

Food: herbivore; grass, dandelions, other green plants in spring and summer; saplings, twigs, bark and other woody plants in winter

Sounds: loud high-pitched scream or squeal when caught by a predator such as a fox or coyote

Breeding: late Feb-Mar mating; 30 days gestation; starts to breed at 3 months

Young: 3-6 offspring up to 5 times per year; born naked and helpless with eyes closed

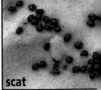

camouflaged

Signs: small woody twigs and branches near the ground are cleanly cut off and at an angle, while browse from deer is higher up and has a ragged edge (due to the lack of upper incisors in deer), bark is stripped off of saplings and shrubs; dry, pea-sized light brown pellets, round and woody; soft green pellets are ingested and rarely seen

scat

Activity: nocturnal, crepuscular; often very active during late winter and early spring when males fight to breed with females

Tracks: hind paw 3-4" (7.5-10 cm) long, forepaw 1" (2.5 cm) long, small and round; 1 set of 4 tracks; forepaws fall one in front of the other behind hind prints

Stan's Notes: The most widespread of the eight cottontail species in North America, seen in the eastern United States, all of Florida and most of Mexico. Transplanted to many areas that historically did not have cottontails. Common name was given for its cotton ball-like tail.

Usually stays in a small area of only a couple acres. Often freezes, hunkers down and flattens ears if danger is near. Quickly runs in a zigzag pattern, circling back to its starting spot when flushed. Able to leap up to 12-15 feet (3.7-4.5 m) in a single bound while running. Also jumps sideways while running to break its scent trail. Uses a set of well-worn trails in winter, usually in thick cover of bushes. Cools itself on hot summer days by stretching out in shaded grassy areas.

Usually not a territorial animal, with fights among males breaking out only during mating season. Interspersed with chasing, males face each other, kick with front feet and jump high into the air.

After mating, the female excavates a small area for a nest, lines it with soft plants and fur from her chest for comfort and camouflages the entrance. Mothers nurse their babies at dawn and dusk. Once the young open their eyes and are moving outside the nest, they are on their

cooling

own and get no further help from their mother. One of the most reproductively successful rabbit species in North America, with some females producing as many as 35 offspring annually; however, most young do not live longer than 1 year.

Like other rabbits and hares, this species produces fecal pellets that are dry and brown or soft and green. Eats the green pellets to regain the nutrition that wasn't digested initially.

Black-tailed Jackrabbit
Lepus californicus

Family: Rabbits and Hares (Leporidae)

Size: L 18-24" (45-61 cm); T 2-3" (5-7.5 cm)

Weight: 4-8 lb. (1.8-3.6 kg)

Description: Gray to light brown in summer with black-tipped hair, giving it a grizzled appearance. Light white belly. Extremely long ears with black tips. Long legs. Large hind feet. Large brown eyes. A large, puffy white tail with black on top, extending to the rump.

Origin/Age: non-native; 1-5 years

Compare: This hare stands much taller than the cottontails (pp. 165-169) and is as tall as a medium-sized domestic dog. Its huge size and large ears make it easy to identify.

Habitat: scrublands, grasslands, airports

Home: shallow nest underneath a bush or other shrub or beneath a log, lined with dry grasses and hair from the mother, uses a burrow in winter

Food: herbivore; green plants in summer, twigs, bark, leaf buds, dried grasses and berries in winter

Sounds: inconsequential; may give a loud, shrill scream when captured by a large predator

Breeding: Feb-May mating; 30-40 days gestation

Young: 1-11 offspring 4-5 times per year; born fully furred with eyes open and incisor teeth erupted, able to move around within an hour of birth

Signs: trails worn between feeding areas and resting sites; hard, dry, woody, slightly flattened, dark brown pellets, ½" (1 cm) wide, or moist green pellets

Activity: mostly nocturnal, crepuscular; can be seen during cloudy or overcast days

Tracks: hind paw 4-5½" (10-14 cm) long and 2" (5 cm) wide, forepaw 1" (2.5 cm) long, small and round; 1 set of 4 tracks; forepaws are slightly offset side by side or fall one in front of the other behind hind prints

Stan's Notes: A common jackrabbit across the western half of the country. Introduced to Florida during the 1920-30s to train greyhound dogs for racing. Now seen in pockets in Florida such as at the Miami International Airport. Sometimes called Jackass Rabbit, although it is actually a type of hare. Hard to misidentify because it is so large and runs with a seesaw-like rocking from the front to hind feet. Black on tail and rump is best seen when it runs. Can leap as far as 20 feet (6.1 m) and run up to 45 mph (72 km/h) for a short distance, slowing to a series of low leaps from 4-10 feet (1.2-3 m).

The enormous ears have a generous blood flow, which dissipates heat during summer. The ears also provide an excellent means of predator detection. The large hind legs facilitate high jumps and quick escapes from predators and are used for defense, kicking and scratching with its claws. Does not like water, but is a good swimmer and may plunge into water to escape a predator.

Usually solitary, but may be seen in large groups, especially in spring when it gathers for mating. Females can be slightly larger than males (bucks), but there are no obvious differences between sexes. When bucks fight, they kick with hind feet and bite.

Rests under logs or other shelter (shade) during the day and will flush only if contact is very close. During winter it snuggles in burrows that may be connected by tunnels, resting with its large ears pressed flat against its back.

Female constructs a simple nest–a shallow depression lined with grasses and fur plucked from her chest. Babies can run within an hour of their birth. They are eating plants at 2 weeks and weaned shortly after, fully independent at 4 weeks. If born early enough in the season, young females can breed before their first winter.

Reingestion of soft fecal pellets (coprophagy) occurs in hares, as it does in rabbits.

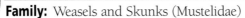

Long-tailed Weasel
Mustela frenata

Family: Weasels and Skunks (Mustelidae)

Size: L 8-16" (20-40 cm); T 3-6" (7.5-15 cm)

Weight: 3-9 oz. (85-255 g)

Description: Light brown with a white-to-yellow chin, throat, chest and belly. Long tubular body. Short legs and brown feet. Long brown tail with a black tip. Some individuals turn all white in winter except for the black-tipped tail. Male slightly larger than the female.

Origin/Age: native; 5-10 years

Compare: Mink (pg. 181) is larger and darker brown, with a small white patch on its chin.

Habitat: wetlands, fields, prairies, farms, edges of mixed forests, grasslands, farms, wet areas

Home: nest made from grass and fur, usually in an old chipmunk, ground squirrel or mole burrow or beneath logs and rocks; often has several nests in its territory

Food: carnivore, insectivore; small to medium mammals such as mice, voles, chipmunks, squirrels and rabbits; will also eat small birds, bird eggs, carrion and insects

Sounds: single loud trills or rapid trills, squeals

Breeding: summer (Jul-Aug) mating; 30-34 days gestation; ova develop for 8 days after fertilization, then cease development, implantation is delayed up to 8-10 months after mating

Young: 4-8 offspring once per year from April to June

Signs: long, thin, often dark scat with a pointed end, contains hair and bones, often on a log or rock, very similar to mink scat

Activity: primarily nocturnal, diurnal mostly during the winter; hunts during the day for several hours, then rests and sleeps for several hours

Tracks: hind paw ¾-1" (2-2.5 cm) long, forepaw slightly smaller, both round with well-defined nail marks, 5 toes on all feet; 1 set of 4 tracks when bounding; 12-20" (30-50 cm) stride

Stan's Notes: Widespread, but rare in Florida. An active predator that runs in a series of bounds with back arched and tail elevated. A good swimmer and will climb trees to pursue squirrels. Quickly locates prey using its excellent eyesight and sense of smell, dashes to grab it, then kills it with several bites to the base of the skull. Favorite foods include mice and voles. Sometimes hunts for larger prey such as rabbits. Eats its fill and caches the rest. Consumes 25-40 percent of its own body weight in food daily.

In Florida and across the southern range, most individuals stay brown and do not turn white in winter.

winter

Uses scents and sounds to communicate with other weasels. Deposits scat on rocks and trails to mark territory. Both sexes apply an oily, odoriferous substance from their anal glands onto rocks, trees and other prominent landmarks to communicate territory, social status, sex and willingness to mate. The odor is rarely detectable by people, especially after a few days. Male territory is 25-55 acres (10-22 ha). Female territory is smaller. Defends territory against other weasels.

Solitary except during mating season and when a mother is with her young. Constructs nest in an abandoned animal burrow or beneath logs and rocks, using grass for nesting material along with the fur of small animals it has eaten.

Mink
Mustela vison

Family: Weasels and Skunks (Mustelidae)

Size: L 14-20" (36-50 cm); T 6-8" (15-20 cm)

Weight: 1½-3½ lb. (.7-1.6 kg)

Description: Dark brown to nearly black or brown to blond, often with a luster. Same color belly and back. Small white patch on chin. Short, round dark ears. Long tubular body with short legs. A long bushy tail, darker near the tip. Male slightly larger than female.

Origin/Age: native; 5-10 years

Compare: Larger than the Long-tailed Weasel (pg. 177), which has lighter brown fur with a white-to-yellow underside.

Habitat: along rivers, lakes and streams, wetlands, farms, forests

Home: burrow, entrance is 4" (10 cm) wide

Food: carnivore; small to medium mammals such as voles, mice, chipmunks, rabbits and squirrels, but favors muskrats; also eats small birds, bird eggs, snakes, frogs, toads, crayfish and fish

Sounds: chatters, scolds, hisses, snarls when alarmed or fighting other minks

Breeding: Jan-Apr mating; 32-51 days gestation; implantation delayed, length of delay is dependent upon when the female mates during the season

Young: 3-6 offspring once per year; born covered with fine hair and eyes closed, eyes open at about 7 weeks, weaned at 8-9 weeks, mature at 5 months

brown morph

scat

Signs: small, thin dark scat, usually pointed at one end, usually containing bone, fur and fish scales, deposited on rocks and logs along lakes and rivers

Activity: nocturnal, diurnal; hunts for several hours, then rests several hours

Tracks: hind paw 2-3¼" (5-8 cm) long with 5 toes, forepaw 1¼-1¾" (3-4.5 cm) long with 5 toes, both round with well-defined nail marks; 1 set of 4 tracks when bounding; 12-25" (30-64 cm) stride; tracks may end at the edge of water

Stan's Notes: Also known as American Mink. Usually seen along the banks of rivers and lakes in Florida. Its thick, oily, waterproof fur provides great insulation and enables the animal to swim in nearly freezing water. Its partially webbed toes aid in swimming. Able to swim underwater as far as 100 feet (30 m) before surfacing. Can dive down to 15 feet (4.6 m) for its favorite food, muskrats.

Hunts on land for chipmunks, rabbits, snakes and frogs. Moves in a series of loping bounds with its back arched and tail held out slightly above horizontal. When frightened or excited, releases an odorous substance from glands near the base of its tail.

Burrow is almost always near water, often under a tree root or in a riverbank. May use a hollow log or muskrat burrow after killing and eating the occupants. Active burrows will often have a strong odor near the entrance. Most burrows are temporary since minks are almost constantly on the move looking for their next meal.

The male maintains a territory of up to 40 acres (16 ha), with the female territory less than half the size. Will mark its territory by applying a pungent discharge on prominent rocks and logs. It is a polygamous breeder.

The pelt of a mink is considered to be one of the most luxurious. Demand for the fur has led to the establishment of mink ranches, where the fur color can be controlled by selective breeding.

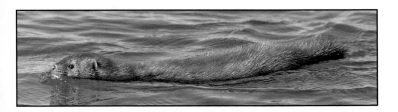

Northern River Otter
Lontra canadensis

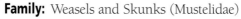

Family: Weasels and Skunks (Mustelidae)

Size: L 2½-3½' (76-107 cm); T 11-20" (28-50 cm)

Weight: 10-30 lb. (4.5-13.5 kg)

Description: Overall dark brown-to-black fur, especially when wet, with a lighter brown-to-gray belly. Silver-to-gray chin and throat. Small ears and eyes. Short snout with white whiskers. Elongated body with a long thick tail, tapered at the tip. Male slightly larger than female.

Origin/Age: native; 7-20 years

Compare: Round-tailed Muskrat (pg. 111) is much smaller and has a long, thin naked tail. American Beaver (pg. 119) has a wide flat tail.

Habitat: rivers, streams, medium to large lakes

Home: permanent and temporary dens

Food: carnivore, insectivore; fish, crayfish, frogs, small mammals, aquatic insects

Sounds: loud shrill cries when threatened, during play will grunt, growl and snort, chuckles when with mate or siblings

Breeding: Mar-Apr mating; 200-270 days gestation; implantation delayed for an unknown amount of time, entire reproduction process may take up to a year, female mates again days after giving birth

Young: 1-6 offspring once per year in March or April; born fully furred with eyes closed, eyes open at around 30 days, weaned at about 3 months

sleeping

Signs: haul outs, slides and rolling areas; scat is dark brown to green, short segments frequently contain fish bones and scales or crayfish parts, deposited on lakeshores, riverbanks, rocks or logs in water

scat

Activity: diurnal, nocturnal; active year-round, spends most of time in water, comes onto land to rest and sleep, curls up like a house cat to sleep

Tracks: hind paw 3½" (9 cm), forepaw slightly smaller, both round with a well-defined heel pad and toes spread evenly apart, 5 toes on all feet; 1 set of 4 tracks when bounding; 12-24" (30-61 cm) stride

Stan's Notes: A large semiaquatic animal seen throughout Florida in major rivers. Well suited to life in the water, with a streamlined body, webbed toes, long guard hairs and dense oily undercoat. Special valves close the nostrils underwater, enabling submersion for up to 6-8 minutes.

A playful, social animal, not often very afraid of people. Can be seen in small groups (mostly mothers with young), swimming and fishing in rivers and lakes. Frequently raises its head high while treading water to survey surroundings. Enjoys sliding on its belly down well-worn areas of mud or grass (slides) along riverbanks or lakeshores just for fun. Can dive to depths of 50 feet (15 m). Sensitive to water pollution, quickly leaving a contaminated area.

Often feeds on slow-moving fish that are easy to catch such as catfish and suckers. Mistakenly blamed for eating too many game fish. Comes to the surface to eat, bringing larger items to eat at the shore. Uses its forepaws to manipulate, carry and tear apart food. Creates haul outs, well-worn trails leading from the water that often end up being littered with fish heads, scat and crayfish parts.

Likes to roll, which flattens areas of vegetation up to 6 feet (1.8 m) wide. Rolling areas have a musky odor from scent marking and usually contain some scat. Very vocal, giving a variety of sounds, such as a loud whistle, to communicate over long distances.

Male defends territory against other males. Female moves freely in and out of male territory. Digs den in a riverbank or lakeshore, often with an underwater entrance. May use an old beaver lodge. Has permanent and temporary dens. Permanent den, lined with leaves, grasses, mosses and hair, usually is where young are born.

Becomes sexually mature at 2-3 years. A male is generally solitary except during mating season and not around for the birth of the young. Returns in midsummer to help raise them.

Eastern Spotted Skunk
Spilogale putorius

Family: Skunks (Mephitidae)

Size: L 13-15" (33-38 cm); T 3-8" (7.5-20 cm)

Weight: 1½-2 lb. (.7-.9 kg)

Description: White spot on the head between the eyes. About 6 white stripes along the back and sides, some broken into dashes and spots. Black tail with a white tip.

Origin/Age: native; 2-5 years

Compare: Striped Skunk (pg. 193) is much larger, lacks spots and has fewer stripes.

Habitat: mixed woodlands, woodland edges, farmlands, river bottoms, suburbs, pine forests

Home: no regular burrow, may use a hollow log or old woodchuck den, area under a deck or porch in summer, digs its own burrow, mostly for winter use; female uses burrow only to give birth

Food: omnivore; voles, mice and other small animals, insects; also eats earthworms, grubs, corn, nuts, berries, seeds and amphibians

Sounds: generally quiet; will stomp front feet and chatter its teeth

Breeding: Feb-Mar mating; 50-65 days gestation; implantation delayed until 2 weeks after mating

Young: 1-6 offspring once per year; born covered in fine black and white fur with eyes and ears closed, eyes and ears open at about 30 days

189

Signs: pungent odor, worse when the animal has sprayed, can be detected even if it has not sprayed; small dark scat, often with a pointed end, deposited on trails and logs

scat

Activity: nocturnal, diurnal; spends the day in a hollow log, brush pile, haystack or wall of a barn or similar building, forages for food mostly on the ground at night

Tracks: hind paw 1¼" (3 cm) long with 5 toes, forepaw 1" (2.5 cm) long with 5 toes, both tracks round with several separate toe and heel pads; 1 set of 4 tracks when bounding; fore and hind prints are very close together, 3-5" (7.5-13 cm) stride

Stan's Notes: Once common in Florida, in most areas this small skunk is now rare. Because one of its main foods is insects, it is thought the widespread use of insecticides is responsible for this dramatic decline.

Considered by some to have the finest, softest fur in the animal world. A semisocial animal, but secretive. Fast, agile and adept at climbing trees. An expert mouser that, like a house cat, is good at controlling small mammal and insect populations around farms. Constantly on the move, looking for its next meal. Much more carnivorous than the Striped Skunk (pg. 193).

Also called Civet Cat, but this is a misleading name because it is neither a civet (mongoose, member of the Viverridae family), nor is it a cat. Species name *putorius* is Latin and refers to the pungent smell of its spray.

When threatened, it rushes forward, stomps its feet and stands on its forepaws with hind end elevated. Agile enough to spray from this position. Can spray up to 10 feet (3 m) with surprising accuracy. Odor is similar to that of the Striped Skunk.

Female matures sexually at 9-11 months. Mother raises the young without any help from the male.

Striped Skunk
Mephitis mephitis

Family: Skunks (Mephitidae)

Size: L 20-24" (50-61 cm); T 7-14" (18-36 cm)

Weight: 6-12 lb. (2.7-5.4 kg)

Description: Variable stripe patterns. Black with a large white stripe from ears to tail, sometimes splitting down the hind quarters. Large bushy tail, shorter or equal to body length, white or black with white sides. Thin white stripe down the center of head between ears and eyes. Male larger than female.

Origin/Age: native; 2-5 years

Compare: The Eastern Spotted Skunk (pg. 189) is much smaller, has spots and more stripes.

Habitat: woodlands, river bottoms, farmlands, woodland edges, prairies, fields, suburban and urban areas

Home: burrow, often in hollow log or tree crevice, under a deck, porch, firewood or rock pile in summer

Food: omnivore; insects, spiders, small mammals, earthworms, grubs, bird eggs, amphibians, corn, fruit, berries, nuts, seeds, reptiles

Sounds: generally quiet; will stomp front feet and exhale in a loud "pfittt," also chatters its teeth

Breeding: Feb-Apr mating; 62-66 days gestation; implantation delayed until 18-20 days after mating

Young: 4-7 offspring once per year; born naked with black and white skin (matching the color of its future fur coat) and eyes closed, musky odor at 8-10 days, eyes open at about 24 days

babies in burrow   juvenile

Signs: pungent odor, more obvious when the skunk has sprayed, can be detected even when it has not sprayed; segmented cylindrical scat, often dark, deposited on trails and at entrance to the den

scat

Activity: mostly nocturnal; more active during summer than winter

Tracks: hind paw 2-3½" (5-9 cm) long with 5 toes and a well-defined heel pad, looking flat-footed, forepaw 1-1¾" (2.5-4.5 cm) long and wide with 5 toes; alternating fore and hind prints are very close together when walking, 4-6" (10-15 cm) stride

Stan's Notes: Found throughout Florida, the United States and well into Canada. Can be highly variable in color and pattern across this large range. Bred in the early 1900s for its fur, which explains the wide variety of colors in pet skunks today. The white stripes of a skunk, which vary in length and width from one animal to another, can be used to identify individuals. Some have such wide stripes that they appear to be all white, although most are not albino.

The prominent black and white markings warn predators that it should not be approached. Will face a predator when threatened, arch its back and raise its tail while chattering its teeth. If this does not deter the predator, it will rush forward, stomp its feet, stand on forepaws with tail elevated and spray an oily, odorous yellow substance from glands at the base of its tail near the anus.

Able to spray 5-6 times up to 15 feet (4.6 m) with surprising accuracy. This substance can cause temporary blindness and intense pain if it enters the eyes. Holding the animal by its tail off the ground will not prevent it from spraying. Genus and species names refer to the spray and mean "bad odor."

This is a solitary, secretive skunk that wanders around in a slow, shuffling waddle in search of food. Does not hibernate, but will hole up in its burrow for a few weeks to two months during cold weather. Known to burrow in groups of up to 15 individuals, often all females. This can be a problem when the burrow is under a house because of the cumulative smell.

spraying

Northern Raccoon
Procyon lotor

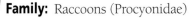

Family: Raccoons (Procyonidae)

Size: L 24-25" (61-64 cm); T 7-16" (18-40 cm)

Weight: 12-35 lb. (5.4-15.8 kg)

Description: Overall gray to brown, sometimes nearly black to silver. Distinctive black band across face (mask), eyes and down to the chin. White snout. Bushy, black-tipped brown tail with 4-6 evenly spaced dark bands or rings.

Origin/Age: native; 6-10 years

Compare: Very distinctive animal. The black mask and dark rings on the tail make it hard to confuse with any other species.

Habitat: almost all habitats, rural and urban, always near water

Home: hollow tree, or underground den where trees are absent

Food: omnivore; crayfish, fish, reptiles, amphibians, nuts, fruit, green leaves, suet, birdseed (especially black-oil sunflower seeds and thistle), small mammals, baby birds, bird eggs, insects

Sounds: very loud snarls, growls, hisses and screams are common (and may be frightening) during the mating season, soft purring sounds and quiet chuckles between mothers and babies

Breeding: Feb-Jun mating; 54-65 days gestation; female in heat (estrus) for only 3-6 days

Young: 3-6 offspring per year, usually in May; born with eyes closed, leaves den at 7-8 weeks

Signs: pile of half-digested berries deposited on a log, rock, under a bird feeder or on top of a garbage can; scat is usually cylindrical, 2" (5 cm) long and ¾" (2 cm) wide, but can be highly variable due to diet

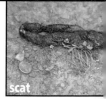

scat

Activity: nocturnal; active year-round except during cold snaps in winter

Tracks: hind paw 3½-4½" (9-11 cm) long with 5 long toes and claw marks, forepaw 2½-3" (6-7.5 cm) long, slightly longer than wide with 5 distinct toes and claw marks; forepaws land (register) next to hind prints, 8-20" (20-50 cm) stride

Stan's Notes: Raccoons are native only to the Americas from Central America to the United States and lower Canada. Northern Raccoon is found across Florida in nearly all habitats. Common name is from the Algonquian Indian word *arougbcoune*, meaning "he scratches with his hands." Known for the ability to open such objects as doors, coolers and latches. Uses its nimble fingers to feel around the edges of ponds, rivers and lakes for crayfish and frogs.

Known to occasionally wash its food before eating, hence the species name *lotor*, meaning "washer." However, it is not washing its food, but kneading and tearing it apart. The water helps it feel the parts that are edible and those that are not. A strong swimmer.

Able to climb any tree very quickly and can come down headfirst or tail end first. Its nails can grip bark no matter which way it climbs because it can rotate its hind feet nearly 180 degrees so that the hind toes always point up the tree.

Active at night, sleeping in hollow trees or other dens during the day. Often mis-

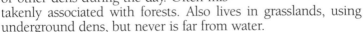

juveniles

takenly associated with forests. Also lives in grasslands, using underground dens, but never is far from water.

Usually solitary as an adult. Does not hibernate but may sleep or simply hole up in a comfortable den in January and February, depending on the weather. Will occasionally den in small groups of the same sex, usually males, or females without young.

Males wander many miles in search of a mate. Females use the same den for several months while raising their young, but move out afterward and find a new place to sleep each night. Males are not involved in raising young. Young remain with the adult female for nearly a year.

White-nosed Coati

Nasua narica

Family: Raccoons (Procyonidae)

Size: L 25-30" (64-76 cm); T 15-27" (38-69 cm)

Weight: 10-25 lb. (4.5-11.3 kg)

Description: Overall light to dark brown, frequently cinnamon, sometimes with a lighter saddle-like shape on the back. Distinctive black facial marks, white around eyes and a white snout. Short, round white ears. Short legs with white on upper part of front legs. Long curved claws. A very long, bushy tail with faint rings, tapering to a point at the end. Holds tail up straight or bent like a question mark.

Origin/Age: non-native; 6-10 years

Compare: Northern Raccoon (pg. 197) has a black mask and shorter ringed tail. The Raccoon is nocturnal (nighttime); Coati is diurnal (daytime), travels in a group (troop) and holds its tail up straight.

Habitat: forests, woodlands, near water

Home: no real home or den, spends the night in trees, daytime on the ground; uses a maternity den in a rock outcrop for birthing

Food: omnivore; fruit, nuts, large insects, amphibians, reptiles, small mammals, baby birds, bird eggs

Sounds: very loud growls and snarls, hisses and whimpers, soft chattering and chirps

Breeding: Jan-Mar mating; 75-77 days gestation

Young: 4-6 offspring once per year, in spring; born with eyes closed, leaves the den at 5-6 weeks, young have darker coats than adults, young males stay with the troop until 2 years of age

sleeping

family group

Signs: pile of half-digested berries deposited on a log or rock; scat is usually cylindrical, 2" (5 cm) long and ¾" (2 cm) wide, but can be highly variable depending on diet

Activity: diurnal; active year-round, sleeps in trees at night

Tracks: hind paw 3-3½" (7.5-9 cm) long with 5 long toes and claw marks, forepaw 2-2½" (5-6 cm) long with 5 distinct toes and very long claw marks; forepaws land (register) behind the hind prints, 7-15" (18-38 cm) stride

Stan's Notes: An interesting relative to the more common and well-known Northern Raccoon (pg. 197). Isolated introduced populations occur in southern Florida. Also known as Antoon, Coatimundi or just Coati (pronounced "ko-WHA-tee"). Called Tejon ("badger") in Mexico. All members of the Raccoons family live in the New World. Coati are seen in Mexico and Central America, with small populations living in southern Texas, New Mexico and Arizona. These appear to be native populations as opposed to being introduced to Florida.

Active during the day, foraging for food in large groups. A group, or troop, consists of up to 50 females and young, but smaller sizes are more common. Females and their young are in groups year-round. Males are solitary except for several weeks during breeding season when they seek receptive females.

Feeds by rooting around in leaf litter for insects, nuts and berries. Climbs trees for fruit and often returns repeatedly until all fruit is gone. A true omnivore, eating whatever food it finds. Feeds in the morning and late in the evening, lowering its tail when feeding.

An excellent climber, using its long tail to help balance on small branches. Travels holding its tail upright. Swims well. Naps and grooms in trees during the day, especially when it is hot.

Sleeps in trees at night to avoid predators. Active all year and does not use a den except when giving birth. Females will use the den with their young for the first 5-6 weeks until the young are strong enough to keep up with the troop.

More gregarious than other members of the Raccoons family and much more vocal. Young play noisily, while adults are most vocal when interacting with each other. Spends time grooming itself and other individuals while giving soft soothing sounds.

Like the raccoon, the coati tolerates people well and will raid camps, garbage cans and parking lots for anything edible. Highly intelligent and able to problem solve and remember tasks.

Nine-banded Armadillo

Dasypus novemcinctus

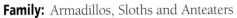

Family: Armadillos, Sloths and Anteaters (Dasypodidae)

Size: L 15-21" (38-53 cm); T 9-14" (23-36 cm)

Weight: 8-17 lb. (3.6-7.7 kg)

Description: Unique-looking round body covered in 9 heavy bony plates (armor). Each scale looks like it is comprised of small scales. Tan to brown, usually covered in mud, but can be shiny. Long, narrow pointed snout. Tiny eyes and tall oval ears. Short legs. Long nails. Long narrow tail, lacking hair.

Origin/Age: native; 4-7 years

Compare: Hard to confuse with any other animal. Opossum (pg. 209) has a furred body. Look for segmented body armor and a hairless tail to help identify.

Habitat: grasslands, open woodlands, scrublands, wetlands

Home: burrow, several entrances with little excavated dirt, sometimes at the base of a rock, usually in a small hill or riverbank, up to 15' (4.5 m) long and 3' (1 m) deep, 1 chamber lined with vegetation

Food: omnivore; mainly insects; also eats the carrion of rabbits, squirrels, snakes, lizards and frogs

Sounds: sniffing noises, several grunts and groans

Breeding: Jul-Aug mating; 115-120 days gestation; implantation delayed until late October or November

Young: up to 6 offspring once per year; born with eyes open and shell intact (but not hardened), young often genetically identical, with quadruplets most commonly produced from a single fertilized egg, weaned at about 3 months

tail

Signs: burrow entrance that is 6-8" (15-20 cm) wide; round gray pellets, ¾" (2 cm) wide, resembling clay marbles due to the amount of soil consumed while digging up insects

Activity: diurnal, nocturnal; can be seen at many times of the day and night, does not come out on cold, rainy days

Tracks: hind paw 2" (5 cm) long with 5 toes, forepaw 1½-1¾" (4-4.5 cm) long, with 4 toes; 1 set of 4 tracks; hind paws fall slightly behind fore prints; tracks often in a straight line, 4-6" (10-15 cm) stride with a partial tail drag mark, seen in dry dirt and mud along streams and wetlands

Stan's Notes: Member of an order of animals with unique back-bone joints that allow more bending than is possible in animals without the special joints. Animals in this group are found only in the New World, in South, Central and North America. There are several armadillo species, but only the Nine-banded is seen in North America. Expanding its range in the United States, having moved up from Mexico.

Historically, several armadillo species populated Florida millions of years ago. The current armadillos are a combination of a wild population moving eastward from Texas and captive individuals that escaped during the 1920-30s.

Gets the common name "Nine" from the number of armored, jointed (articulated) plates on its body. Able to curl up into a tight ball, with the plate on top of its head protecting the joint where the front and back of the armored shell meet. When threatened, the first defense of an armadillo is to run off or hide in its burrow, where it lodges itself, using its armor as protection. Armored up inside a burrow makes it nearly impossible to pull the animal out. If the burrow is not near, it will roll up into an impenetrable ball.

Eyesight is not that great, so sometimes it stands upright to sniff the air for danger, supporting itself with its tail. Spends most of its time out of the burrow with its nose to the ground, sniffing for insects or other food. An excellent excavator, digging under fallen logs or tearing apart logs, using its short, thick, powerful legs and long toe nails to burrow and search out food. A desirable animal to have around due to the large number of insects it consumes at ranches and farms.

Young can walk within hours of birth. Appearing like miniature piglets, they follow their mother around in a line, single file.

in pouch

Signs: overturned garbage cans; scat on ground under sunflower seed and Nyjer thistle feeders

Activity: nocturnal; can be seen during the day in winter

scat

Tracks: hind paw 2" (5 cm) long with 5 toes, large thumb-like first toe points inward and lacks a nail, forepaw 1½" (4 cm) long with 5 toes spread out; fore and hind prints are parallel, 7" (18 cm) stride, often has a tail drag mark

Stan's Notes: This is the only marsupial found north of Mexico. A unique-looking, interesting animal, the size of a house cat. It has 50 teeth, more than any other mammal in Florida. Usually solitary, moving around on the ground from place to place. Also climbs trees well, using its tail to aid in climbing, holding onto branches (semiprehensile). An adult opossum cannot hang by the tail like a monkey, but the young seem able to, perhaps due to their lighter weight.

Frequently feeds on dead animals along roads and is often hit by vehicles. Not a fast mover, it will hiss if threatened and show its short, pointy teeth. When that doesn't work, it often will roll over and feign death with eyes closed, mouth open and tongue hanging out, "playing 'possum."

Does not hibernate, but sleeps in dens for weeks during the coldest part of winter.

playing 'possum

Males give loud, aggressively displays during the breeding season and will scent-mark by licking themselves and rubbing their heads against tree trunks or other stationary objects. Young ride on their mother's back after weaning.

Opossums can defend themselves against large predators and survive substantial injuries. One study showed nearly half of all examined dead opossums had healed broken bones, some with multiple fractures. Many opossums are immune to venomous snake bites and have a resistance to rabies and plague.

Gray Fox
Urocyon cinereoargenteus

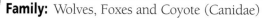

Family: Wolves, Foxes and Coyote (Canidae)

Size: L 22-24" (56-61 cm); T 10-17" (25-43 cm); H 14-15" (36-38 cm)

Weight: 7-13 lb. (3.2-5.9 kg)

Description: Grizzled gray fox with a rust red nape, shoulders and rust red across the chest. Large pointed ears, trimmed in white. White chin, neck and belly. Large bushy tail with a black tip and ridge of stiff dark hairs along the top.

Origin/Age: native; 5-10 years

Compare: The Red Fox (pg. 217) has a white-tipped tail. Coyote (pg. 221) shares the grayish appearance and black-tipped tail, but is larger than the Gray Fox and has longer legs.

Habitat: deciduous forests, pine forests, river valleys, brushy areas, suburban and urban areas

Home: den, mostly in a natural cavity such as a log or a crevice in rock, will enlarge a prairie dog burrow, unlike a Red Fox den, the den of a Gray Fox lacks a mound of dirt in front of the entrance

Food: omnivore; small mammals such as mice, moles, voles, rabbits and hares; also eats berries, apples, nuts, fish, insects and carrion

Sounds: hoarse high-pitched barks, yelps to steady high-pitched screams, mournful cries; much less vocal than the Red Fox

Breeding: winter (Jan-Mar) mating; 51-53 days gestation

Young: 1-7 kits once per year in April or May; born helpless with black fur and eyes closed

Signs: urine and piles of feces, mostly on conspicuous landmarks such as a prominent rock, stump or trail; cylindrical scat with a tapered end, can be very dark if berries were eaten, often contains hair and bones

Activity: mostly nocturnal, crepuscular; can be seen during the day in winter, especially when overcast

Tracks: forepaw 1½" (4 cm) long, oval, hind paw slightly smaller; straight line of single tracks; hind paws fall near or directly onto fore prints (direct register) when walking, often obliterating the forepaw tracks, 10-14" (25-36 cm) stride when walking

Stan's Notes: Gray Fox is common across Florida except for the Keys. It dens in woodpiles, fallen trees, culverts and abandoned buildings.

The scientific name provides a very good description of the animal. The genus *Urocyon* is Greek for "tailed dog." The species *cinereoargenteus* is Latin and means "silver" or "gray and black."

Also called Treefox because it often climbs trees. Climbs to escape larger predators more than it does to find food. Sometimes it will rest in a tree. Shinnies up, pivoting its front legs at the shoulder joints to grab the trunk and pushes with hind feet. Able to rotate its front legs more than other canids. Once up the trunk, it jumps from branch to branch and has been seen up to 20 feet (6.1 m) high. Descends by backing down or running headfirst down a sloping branch.

Thought to mate for life. Male often travels 50 miles (81 km) to establish territory. A pair will defend a territory of 2-3 square miles (5-8 sq. km).

The kits are weaned at about six weeks. Male doesn't enter the den, but helps feed the family by bringing in food. Young disperse at the end of summer just before the parents start mating again.

Red Fox
Vulpes vulpes

Family: Wolves, Foxes and Coyote (Canidae)

Size: L 22-24" (56-61 cm); T 13-17" (33-43 cm); H 15-16" (38-40 cm)

Weight: 7-15 lb. (3.2-6.8 kg)

Description: Usually rusty red with dark highlights, but can vary from light yellow to black. Large pointed ears trimmed in black with white inside. White jowls, chest and belly. Legs nearly black. Large bushy tail with a white tip. Fluffy coat in winter and spring. Molts by June, appearing smaller and thinner.

Origin/Age: native; 5-10 years

Compare: Gray Fox (pg. 213) is not as red and has a black-tipped tail. Smaller than the Coyote (pg. 221), usually more red and has a white-tipped tail. All other wild canids lack a tail with a white tip.

Habitat: woodlands, rangelands, grasslands, prairies, pine forests, deciduous forests, suburbs, cities

Home: den, sometimes a hollow log, may dig a den under a log or a rock in a bank of a stream or in a hillside created when land was cut to build a road, often has a mound of dirt up to 3' (.9 m) high in front of the main entrance with scat deposits

Food: omnivore; small mammals such as mice, moles, voles, rabbits and hares; also eats berries, apples, nuts, fish, insects and carrion

Sounds: hoarse high-pitched barks, yelps to steady high-pitched screams, mournful cries

Breeding: winter (Jan-Mar) mating; 51-53 days gestation

Young: 1-10 kits once per year in April or May

summer coat

winter coat

silver morph

dark morph

scat

Signs: cylindrical scat with a tapered end, can be very dark if berries were eaten, frequently contains hair and bones, often found on a trail, prominent rock or stump or at den entrance

Activity: mainly nocturnal, crepuscular; rests during the middle of the night

Tracks: forepaw 2" (5 cm) long, oval, with hind paw slightly smaller; straight line of single tracks; hind paws fall near or directly onto fore prints (direct register) when walking, often obliterating the forepaw tracks, 10-14" (25-36 cm) stride when walking

Stan's Notes: This is the most widely distributed wild canid in the world, ranging across North America, Europe, Asia and northern Africa. Some European Red Foxes were introduced into North America in the 1790s, resulting in confusion about the original distribution and lineage. Formerly found only in the northern quarter of the state, but it has expanded its range southward to the rest of Florida except for the Keys.

den entrance

Usually alone. Very smart and learns from experience. Behaves like a cat, pouncing onto prey. Curls into a ball and sleeps at the base of a tree or rock, even in winter.

Hunts for mice, moles and other small prey by stalking, looking and listening. Hearing differs from the other mammals. Hears low-frequency sounds, enabling it to detect small animals digging and gnawing underground. Chases larger prey such as rabbits and squirrels. Hunts even if full, caching extra food underground. Finds cached food by memory and using its sense of smell.

While mated pairs actively defend their territory from other foxes, they are often killed by coyotes or wolves. Uses a den only several weeks for birthing and raising young. Parents bring food to kits in the den. At first, parents regurgitate the food. Later they bring fresh meat and live prey to the den, where the kits practice killing. Young are dispersed at the end of their first summer, with the males (dog foxes) traveling 100-150 miles (161-242 km)–much farther than females (vixens)–to establish their own territories.

kits

Coyote
Canis latrans

Family: Wolves, Foxes and Coyote (Canidae)

Size: L 3-3½' (.9-1.1 m); T 12-15" (30-38 cm); H 18-24" (45-61 cm)

Weight: 20-40 lb. (9-18 kg)

Description: Tan fur with black and orange highlights. Large, pointed reddish orange ears with white interior. Long narrow snout with a white upper lip. Long legs and bushy black-tipped tail.

Origin/Age: native; 5-10 years

Compare: Smaller than the Red Wolf (pg. 225), with larger ears and a narrower pointed snout. The Red Fox (pg. 217) has black legs and a white-tipped tail.

Habitat: all habitats, rural, suburban and urban areas, forests, fields, farms

Home: den, usually in a riverbank, hillside, under a rock or tree root, entrance 12-24" (30-61 cm) high, can be up to 30' (9.1 m) deep and ends in small chamber where female gives birth; female may dig own den or enlarge a fox or badger den

Food: omnivore; small mammals, reptiles, amphibians, birds, bird eggs, insects, fruit, carrion

Sounds: barks like a dog, calls to others result in a chorus of high-pitched howling and yipping; sounds different from the lower, deeper call of the Red Wolf, which rarely yips

Breeding: mid to late winter; 63 days average gestation

Young: 4-6 pups once per year in April or May; born with eyes closed

221

summer coat

scat

Signs: cylindrical scat (shape is similar to that of domestic dog excrement), often containing fur and bones, along well-worn game trails, on prominent rocks and at trail intersections

Activity: nocturnal, crepuscular, diurnal; can be seen for several hours after sunrise and before sunset

Tracks: forepaw 2¼ (5.5 cm) long, round to slightly oval, hind paw slightly smaller; straight line of single tracks; hind paws fall near or directly onto fore prints (direct register) when walking, often obliterating the forepaw tracks, 12-15" (30-38 cm) stride when walking, 24-30" (61-76 cm) stride when running

Stan's Notes: Sometimes called Brush Wolf or Prairie Wolf, even though this animal is obviously not a wolf. The genus name *Canis* is Latin for "dog." The species name *latrans* is also Latin and means "barking." It is believed that the common name "Coyote" comes from the Aztec word *coyotl*, which means "barking dog."

Not seen east of the Mississippi River until the 1950s. Now occurs in every state. Seen mainly in northern Florida and increasingly in southern Florida. Often viewed as a gluttonous outlaw, but it is only guilty of surviving a rapidly changing environment and outright slaughter by people. Intelligent and playful, much like the domestic dog. Hunts alone or in small groups. Uses its large ears to hear small mammals beneath vegetation.

Most coyotes run with their tails down unlike dogs and wolves, which run with their tails level to upright. A fast runner, it can travel 25-30 mph (40-48 km/h). May reach 40 mph (64 km/h) for short distances. Some coyotes tracked with radio collars are known to travel more than 400 miles (644 km) over several days.

Usually courts for 2-3 months before breeding. A monogamous animal, with mated pairs staying together for many years or for life.

Pups emerge from the den at 2-3 weeks and are weaned at 5-7 weeks. Mother will move her pups from the den when she feels threatened. Mother often gets help raising young from other group members and her mate. Pups do not return to the den once they are able to survive on their own. Mother abandons the den once the pups leave and will often return year after year in spring to use the same den.

FORMER
RANGE

Red Wolf
Canis rufus

Family: Wolves, Foxes and Coyote (Canidae)

Size: L 4-4½' (1.2-1.4 m); T 14-17" (36-43 cm); H 24-36" (61-91 cm)

Weight: 40-80 lb. (18-36 kg)

Description: Usually gray with dark highlights. Reddish tinge, especially on upper legs and face. Large bushy tail, black-tipped. Long pointed ears, widely spaced, with rusty backs. Narrow muzzle and large nose pad. Wide band of white around lips. Long legs and large feet. Male is slightly larger than female.

Origin/Age: native; 5-15 years

Compare: Coyote (pg. 221) is smaller, with shorter legs and a narrow white lip mark. Red Wolf often holds its tail straight out when traveling, while Coyote holds its tail downward.

Habitat: forests, brushlands, grasslands, coastal prairies

Home: shelter or den only for raising young, den can be 5-15' (1.5-4.6 m) deep, frequently more than 1 entrance, fan of dirt at entrance, often scattered bones and fur laying about; used for many years

Food: omnivore; mice, rabbits, hares, deer and bears; also eats berries, grass, insects and fish

Sounds: barks and howls, low deep howling may rise and fall in pitch or remain the same; rarely has a series of yips or yelps at the end, like the Coyote

Breeding: Jan-Feb mating; 63-65 days gestation

Young: 2-5 pups once a year; born helpless, eyes closed

Signs: scrapes in the dirt, urine on posts, rocks and stumps; scat looks like the excrement of a domestic dog, but it is larger and contains hairs and bone fragments

scat

Activity: nocturnal, more diurnal in winter

Tracks: forepaw 5½-6½" (14-16 cm) long, hind paw slightly smaller, both round with clear claw marks; straight line of single tracks; hind paws fall near or directly onto fore prints (direct register) when walking, often obliterating the forepaw tracks, 15-30" (38-76 cm) stride; rarely walks along roads like a domestic dog

Stan's Notes: Once ranged from Illinois to eastern Texas, east to the tip of Florida and up the coast to New England. Eliminated from Florida in the early 1900s due to land use changes over the years and persecution by people. During the 1970s, the last of the remaining 17 Red Wolves were taken into captivity to start a breeding program. Since then, several populations have been reestablished in the wild on St. Vincent Island, off the panhandle.

With so many coyotes in Florida, it seems most likely the animals sighted are actually coyotes. It is believed the success of the coyote is due to it filling the niche that the Red Wolf once occupied.

The entire wild population of Red Wolf, nearly 100 individuals, is in North Carolina. Reintroduction into North Carolina began in the late 1980s along the Great Smoky Mountains. A small population is kept in captivity for reintroduction purposes.

Like other wolf species, the Red Wolf travels great distances in its territory. Consumes 2-5 pounds (.9-2.3 kg) of meat per day, but can go for weeks without food. Feeds mainly on small mammals such as rabbits, rats, mice, raccoons and birds.

Runs in small packs. Packs have a well-defined hierarchy, with one male leader, called alpha, and his female mate, also alpha. Young are subordinate to adults and make up the rest of the pack. Young Red Wolves of the previous year do not help raise the young of the new year.

Jaguarundi
Herpailurus yagouaroundi

Family: Cats (Felidae)

Size: L 27-33" (69-84 cm); T 12-20" (30-50 cm); H 13-19" (33-48 cm)

Weight: 10-20 lb. (4.5-9 kg)

Description: A uniformly colored cat that occurs in 2 distinct colors, reddish brown or gray, which sometimes appears black. Small, flattened, elongated head and small pointed ears. Long tail, matching the color of fur on the body. Silver-tipped fur of the dark morph gives it a grizzled appearance.

Origin/Age: non-native; 7-15 years

Compare: Similar size as Bobcat (pg. 233), which is much more common, has tufts on its ears and lacks the long tail.

Habitat: many habitats such as fields, pine forests and ranchlands

Home: den for giving birth, often in a hollow log, rock crevice or under a pile of tree branches filled with leaves

Food: carnivore; small mammals such as mice, squirrels, rabbits, birds, reptiles, amphibians

Sounds: usually silent, but gives typical cat-like sounds in response to danger or threats, meows and yowls

Breeding: any time of year; 65-70 days gestation

Young: 1-3 (usually 2) kittens 1-2 times per year

dark morph

Signs: claw scratches on posts up to 24-36" (30-91 cm) tall, scent posts marked with urine; cylindrical scat up to 1-2" (2.5-5 cm) long and ¼" (.6 cm) wide, contains hair and bones

Activity: nocturnal, diurnal; rests for several hours during the day, especially if it is hot, in a sheltered spot such as under a fallen log, beneath a shrub or in a rock crevice

Tracks: forepaw and hind paw 1½-1¾" (4-4.5 cm), round, heel pad smooth, toes evenly spread, lacking claw marks; straight line of tracks; hind paws fall close to or onto the fore prints (direct register) when walking, often obliterating forepaw tracks, 6-9" (15-23 cm) stride

Stan's Notes: A small cat with a unique shape, having a flattened, elongated head and shorter front legs than hind legs, making it look as though it is perpetually going downhill. Not well studied, so solid biological information is in short supply. However, the genus, formerly *Felis*, has been changed to *Herpailurus*.

Very secretive, with a range from South and Central America into southern Arizona and Texas. Any jaguarundi in Florida is a result of introduced animals. The first was in 1942 at Chiefland and Hillsborough River State Park. It's never been proven that a viable breeding population exists in the state. Only sporadic sightings have ever been reported in Florida.

There are no populations north of Mexico, but occasionally a single jaguarundi is seen. It is possible that some of these are the offspring of feral house cats. There are also reports of captive jaguarundi escaping and living in the wild.

Apparently does not mind water and occasionally swims to cross rivers. Solitary throughout most of the year, with males seeking females for mating.

One of the few cat species in which offspring of the same litter can be different color morphs. Kittens are born with light spots, which soon fade with age.

Bobcat
Lynx rufus

Family: Cats (Felidae)

Size: L 2¼-3½' (69-107 cm); T 3-7" (7.5-18 cm); H 18-24" (45-61 cm)

Weight: 14-30 lb. (6.3-13.5 kg)

Description: Tawny brown during summer. Light gray during winter with dark streaks and spots. Long stiff fur projects down from jowls and tapers to a point (cheek ruffs). Triangular ears, tipped with short black hairs (tufts). Prominent white spot on the back of ears. Dark horizontal barring on upper legs. Short stubby tail with a black tip on the top and sides and a white underside. Male slightly larger than female.

Origin/Age: native; 10-15 years

Compare: Much smaller than Florida Panther (pg. 237), which has a long rope-like tail. The Jaguarundi (pg. 229) is smaller and not regularly seen in Florida. Look for ear tufts and a white underside of tail to help identify the Bobcat.

Habitat: wide variety, mixed forests, fields, farmlands, suburban areas, cities

Home: den, often in a hollow log, rock crevice or under a pile of tree branches filled with leaves

Food: carnivore; medium to small mammals such as rabbits and mice; also eats birds and carrion

Sounds: raspy meows and yelps, purrs when content

Breeding: Feb-Mar mating; 60-70 days gestation

Young: 1-7 (usually 3) kittens once per year in April or May

233

mother and young

scat

Signs: scratching posts with claw marks 3-4' (.9-1.2 m) aboveground, caches of larger kills covered with a light layer of leaves and twigs, scent posts marked with urine; long cylindrical scat, contains hair and bones, often buried, sometimes visible beneath a thin layer of dirt and debris

Activity: nocturnal, diurnal; often rests on hot days in a sheltered spot such as under a fallen log or in a rock crevice

Tracks: forepaw and hind paw 2" (5 cm), round, multi-lobed heel pad, 4 toes on all feet, lacking claw marks; straight line of tracks; hind paws fall near or on fore prints (direct register) when walking, often obliterating forepaw tracks, 9-13" (23-33 cm) stride

Stan's Notes: This is the most common wildcat species in the country and Florida. Thrives in nearly all habitat types, even on coastal islands. The common name refers to the short, stubby or "bobbed" tail. Frequently walks with tail curled upward, which exposes the white underside, making this animal easy to identify. Makes sounds similar to a house cat.

Often uses the same trails in its territory to patrol for rabbits, which is its favorite food, and other prey. Does not climb trees as much as the Florida Panther (pg. 237), but swims well. Hunts by stalking or laying in wait to attack (ambushing). Ambushes prey by rushing forward, chases and captures it, then kills it with a bite to the neck. Has been known to go without eating for several weeks during periods of famine.

Male has a larger territory than female. Usually solitary except for mating and when mothers are with young. Male will seek out a female in heat. Several males may follow a female until she is ready for mating.

Female does not breed until her second year. She has a primary (natal) den in which kittens are born and live for a short time after birth. Female also has secondary dens in her territory, where she may move her young if the natal den is disturbed. Dens are used only by the females and young. Mother raises young on her own.

kittens

Kittens are born well furred and with spots. Their eyes are closed at birth and open at about 10 days. They are weaned at approximately 8 weeks, when they start to hunt with their mother. Young stay with their mother until about 7 months, when she disperses them to mate.

Florida Panther
Puma concolor conyi

Family: Cats (Felidae)

Size: L 5-6' (1.5-1.8 m); T 24-36" (61-91 cm); H 30-36" (76-91 cm)

Weight: M 80-267 lb. (36-120 kg); F 64-142 lb. (29-64 kg)

Description: Overall light to tawny brown with light gray-to-white underside. White upper lip and chin, pink nose, dark spot at base of white whiskers. Small oval ears. Long legs. Large round feet. Long rope-like tail with a dark tip.

Origin/Age: native; 10-20 years

Compare: Bobcat (pg. 233) is much smaller, with a short tail. Look for a long rope-like tail to help identify the Florida Panther.

Habitat: river valleys, woodlands, unpopulated locations

Home: den, often a sheltered rock crevice, thicket, cave or other protected place; female uses den only to give birth, male does not use den

Food: carnivore; larger mammals such as hares, rabbits, opossums, raccoons, skunks and deer

Sounds: purrs when content or with cubs, growls, snarls and hisses when threatened or in defense, loud frightening scream during mating, rarely roars

Breeding: year-round mating; 90-100 days gestation

Young: 1-6 (usually 3) cubs every 2 years; born helpless and blind, covered with dark spots until 3 months, leaves den at 40-70 days and does not return, remains with mother until 15 months

237

cubs

scat

Signs: long scratches and gashes above 5' (1.5 m) on larger tree trunks, small piles of urine-soaked dirt and debris (serving as scent posts), caches of uneaten prey covered with small branches and leaves; large cylindrical scat up to 10" (25 cm) long and 2" (5 cm) wide, contains hair and bones, sometimes lightly covered with dirt

Activity: primarily nocturnal, to a lesser extent crepuscular; active all year, usually rests in a tree in daytime, rests near a recent kill

Tracks: forepaw and hind paw 5-6" (13-15 cm), round, lobed heel pad, toes evenly spread, lacks claw marks; straight line of tracks; hind paws fall near or onto fore prints (direct register) when walking, often obliterating forepaw tracks, 12-28" (30-71 cm) stride

Stan's Notes: The Florida Panther is a unique subspecies of the western Cougar or Mountain Lion. Only a handful of Florida Panthers exist today, with much effort underway to reestablish the population. So far it has had limited success. Seen only rarely in southern parts of the state. Often secretive and avoids people.

Contrary to the popular belief that it harms the deer population, it usually hunts and kills only about once each week, feeding for many days on the same kill. It hunts by stalking and springing from cover or dropping from a tree. Frequently drags its kill to a secluded area to eat, buries the carcass and returns to feed over the next couple days, often at night. It is an excellent climber and can leap distances up to 20 feet (6.1 m). Will swim if necessary.

Some people mistakenly think this cat will make a good pet and do not know what to do when their "pet" starts to knock down family members and bite them. These "pets" are released and then often turn up in suburban areas. Usually these are the animals that attack people since they have lost their fear of humans.

Home range of the male is 54-115 square miles (140-299 sq. km) and excludes other male panthers. Female range is nearly half the size of the male territory.

Solitary animal except for females with cubs and when mating. During that time the male travels and sleeps with the female for up to a couple weeks. The female matures sexually at 2-3 years of age. Only the females raise the young.

male

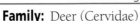

Key Deer
Odocoileus virginianus clavium

Family: Deer (Cervidae)

Size: L 24-36" (61-91 cm); T 4-6" (10-15 cm); H 24" (61 cm)

Weight: M 70-75 lb. (32-34 kg); F 50-55 lb. (23-25 kg)

Description: Reddish brown in summer, yellowish brown in winter. Medium-sized ears, a third the length of the head, white to gray inside with some black. A white eye-ring, nose band, chin, throat and belly. Brown tail with varying amounts of black, and white underside. Male antlers have 1-4 small tines originating from a central beam and a 12-16" (30-40 cm) spread. Female is 20 percent smaller, with a thinner neck and lacks antlers.

Origin/Age: native; 5-10 years

Compare: A tiny deer, hard to confuse with any other.

Habitat: many habitats such as pine woods, scrublands and palmetto thickets; only on the Keys

Home: no den or nest; sleeps in a different spot every night, beds may be concentrated in one area, does not use a shelter in bad weather

Food: herbivore; grasses and other green plants, acorns and nuts in summer, twigs and buds in winter

Sounds: loud whistle-like snorts, male grunts, fawn bleats

Breeding: Sep-Oct mating; 6-7 months gestation

Young: 1-2 fawns once per year in April or May; covered with white spots, walks within hours of birth

mother and fawn   female

Signs: browsed twigs that are ripped or torn (due to the lack of upper incisor teeth), tree rubs (saplings scraped or stripped of bark) made by male while polishing antlers during the rut, oval depressions in grass or leaves are evidence of beds; round, hard brown pellets during winter, segmented cylindrical masses of scat in spring and summer

Activity: nocturnal, crepuscular; moves along same trails to visit feeding areas, most active in early morning and the end of day

Tracks: front hoof 1" (2.5 cm) long, hind hoof ¾-1" (2-2.5 cm), both with a split heart shape with the point in the front; neat line of single tracks; hind hooves fall near or directly onto fore prints (direct register) when walking

Stan's Notes: This small deer is a subspecies of White-tailed Deer (pg. 245) and is seen only on Big Pine Key and surrounding Keys. Wanders around the Keys in yards and unfortunately onto streets, where many are hit and killed each year. Residents dogs have been known to harass Key Deer, biting and tearing at their tails until they are tattered or torn off altogether. Able to run up to 25 mph (40 km/h). Also an excellent swimmer.

The Key Deer are like mainland deer. Male antlers are covered with a furry skin, called velvet, during spring and summer. Velvet contains a network of blood vessels that supplies nutrients to growing antlers. New antler growth begins after the male (buck) drops his antlers in January or February. Some females (does) grow antlers. Antler growth is tied to available nutrition. It is impossible to judge the age of a buck by the number of antler tines or antler size due to the direct correlation between antlers and nutrition. Examining teeth is a better way to estimate age.

This subspecies has been isolated on the Keys for so long, it is becoming distinct from other species of deer. It is limited only by the amount of fresh water it can find to drink and the suitable habitats remaining on the Keys. New housing and development is a constant pressure on Key Deer. Usually restricts its movement to a relatively small home range and is dependent on the location of the food and freshwater supply.

The buck is solitary in spring and early summer, but seeks other bucks in late summer and early fall to spar. Bucks are polygamous. The largest, most dominant bucks mate with many does.

For a couple weeks after birth, fawns lay still all day while their mother is away feeding. Mother nurses them during the evening and at night.

male

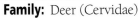

White-tailed Deer
Odocoileus virginianus

Family: Deer (Cervidae)

Size: L 4-7' (1.2-2.1 m); T 6-12" (15-30 cm); H 3-4' (.9- 1.2 m)

Weight: M 100-250 lb. (45-113 kg); F 75-150 lb. (34-68 kg)

Description: Reddish brown during summer, grayish brown during winter. Large ears, white inside with black edges. A white eye-ring, nose band, chin, throat and belly. Brown tail with a black tip and white underside. Male antlers have many small tines originating from a central beam; antler spread is 12-24" (30-61 cm). Female is overall smaller, has a thinner neck and lacks antlers.

Origin/Age: native; 5-10 years

Compare: Sambar Deer (pg. 249) is larger, darker and seen only on St. Vincent Island. Key Deer (pg. 241) is restricted to only a few islands in the Keys.

Habitat: many habitats such as woodlands, ranchlands, wetlands and scrublands

Home: no den or nest; sleeps in a different spot every night, beds may be concentrated in one area, does not use a shelter in bad weather

Food: herbivore; grasses and other green plants, acorns and nuts in summer, twigs and buds in winter

Sounds: loud whistle-like snorts, male grunts, fawn bleats

Breeding: late Aug-Oct mating in southern Florida, Oct-Dec in northern Florida; 6-7 months gestation

Young: 1-2 fawns once per year from April through June; rare to have 3-4; covered with white spots, walks within hours of birth

young male

tree rub female

scat

Signs: browsed twigs that are ripped or torn (due to the lack of upper incisor teeth), tree rubs (saplings scraped or stripped of bark) made by male while polishing antlers during the rut, oval depressions in grass or leaves are evidence of beds; round, hard brown pellets during winter, segmented cylindrical masses of scat in spring and summer

Activity: nocturnal, crepuscular; moves along same trails to visit feeding areas, most active in early morning and the end of day

Tracks: front hoof 2-3" (5-7.5 cm) long, hind hoof slightly smaller, both with a split heart shape with the point in the front; neat line of single tracks; hind hooves fall near or directly onto fore prints (direct register) when walking

Stan's Notes: There are many subspecies of White-tailed Deer in Florida, including the tiny Key Deer (pg. 241), which inhabits just the Keys. All subspecies look similar and act the same; size and habitat are the only differences.

fawn

In summer, antlers are covered with a furry skin known as velvet. Velvet contains a network of blood vessels that supplies nutrients to growing antlers. New antler growth begins after the male (buck) drops his antlers in January or February. Some females (does) grow antlers. Antler growth is tied to available nutrition. It is impossible to judge the age of a buck by the number of antler tines or antler size due to the direct correlation between antlers and nutrition. Examining teeth is a better way to estimate age.

Grows longer guard hairs in winter, giving the deer an overall gray color and larger appearance than in summer. Hairs of the winter coat are thick, hollow and provide excellent insulation.

Usually restricts its movement to a relatively small home range and is dependent on the location of the food supply. Eats 5-9 pounds (2.3-4.1 kg) of food per day, preferring acorns in fall and fresh grass and other green leaves in spring. Research shows that Whitetails eat up to 500 different plants. The four-chambered stomach enables the deer to get nutrients from poor food sources, such as twigs, and eat and drink substances that are unsuitable for people, including poison ivy and deadly mushrooms.

Able to run up to 37 mph (60 km/h), jump up to 8½ feet (2.6 m) high and leap 30 feet (9.1 m). Also an excellent swimmer.

For two weeks after birth, fawns lay still all day while their mother is away feeding. Mother nurses them during the evening and at night.

male

Sambar Deer
Cervus unicolor

Family: Deer (Cervidae)

Size: L 6-7' (1.8-2.1 m); T 10-12" (25-30 cm); H 4-5' (1.2-1.5 m)

Weight: M 600-700 lb. (270-315 kg); F 400-500 lb. (180-225 kg)

Description: Dark brown during summer with gray overtones in winter. Lighter brown on the inside of legs, on the chin and under tail. Male has a thick mane on neck when in rut. Male has thin antlers with basal times, 1 pointing forward, 1 pointing back. Several tines branch from a main beam, usually 3 points on each side. Female is smaller, lighter brown and lacks antlers and a mane.

Origin/Age: non-native; 20-25 years

Compare: Larger than White-tailed Deer (pg. 245), which is not as dark and lacks a mane.

Habitat: woodlands, swamps, open wet meadows, ranches

Home: no den or nest; sleeps in a different spot every night, beds may be concentrated in one area, does not use a shelter in bad weather or winter

Food: herbivore; aquatic plants, grasses and green leaves during summer, woody browse in winter

Sounds: male gives a loud bellow during rut

Breeding: Sep-Jan mating; 9 months gestation

Young: 1 fawn once every 2 years; walks within hours of birth, has reddish brown fur with white spots

mother and fawn

Signs: grass or other green plants cut off low to the ground, beds or flattened areas in the grass indicating resting or sleeping, often under trees; scat is similar to that of White-tailed Deer (pg. 245), only it is larger and there is more of it

Activity: nocturnal, crepuscular; most active in early morning and again at the end of daylight, active into the night for a couple hours

Tracks: front hoof 5-6" (13-15 cm) long, hind hoof 5" (13 cm), both with a split heart shape with the point in the front; neat line of tracks; hind hooves fall near or directly onto fore prints (direct register) when walking

Stan's Notes: A large deer that is more closely related to elk than deer. In fact, it appears more like an elk than a deer. Sambar Deer have rudimentary canine teeth on their upper jaw—unusual since canines are usually found only in meat-eating mammals.

The common name "Sambar" is used for many species of large dark brown deer with thick manes found in Asia, India and other parts of the world. Originally comes from southern Asia, India, southern China, the East Indies, Sumatra, Borneo and Indonesia. It was introduced to many parts of the world such as Australia, New Zealand and southern parts of the United States, including Texas and California.

In Florida it was imported as a game species to St. Vincent Island in 1908, when the island was privately owned. Currently there are fewer than 100 individuals on the island, which is now a national wildlife refuge. Each year a limited hunting season is offered. Seen as one of the most elusive game species and highly prized due to its large size.

Highly variable in color and size, with many subspecies. Most varieties are smaller, lighter brown and do not occur in Florida. Usually does not herd, but can be seen in small groups of females and young. Males are solitary.

Wild Hog
Sus scrofa

Family: Old World Swine (Suidae)

Size: L 4-6' (1.2-1.8 m); T 6-12" (15-30 cm); H 2-3' (61-91 cm)

Weight: M 200-400 lb. (90-180 kg); F 75-300 lb. (34-135 kg)

Description: Extremely variable in color from dark brown and black to gray and white. Large thick body, long pointed snout and short dark legs. Thick fur and well-furred ears. Tail is furred and hangs straight down. Tusks up to 9" (23 cm) long, curling out alongside of mouth. Tiny dark eyes. Female has the same colors, but is smaller and lacks tusks.

Origin/Age: non-native; 15-20 years

Compare: No other pig-like animal occurs in the wilds of Florida.

Habitat: open forests, ranches, farms

Home: no den or nest, rests out in the open or in open forests; female does not seek shelter to give birth, but makes a bed for birthing not far from water

Food: omnivore; grasses and other green plants, insects, mammals, reptiles, amphibians, birds

Sounds: snorts and grunts similar to domestic pigs

Breeding: year-round mating; 16 weeks gestation

Young: 5-7 piglets twice per year; only 6-8" (15-20 cm) at birth, usually brown with pale longitudinal body stripes, able to walk and follow mother at 1 week, nurses for 3 months

Signs: large holes in the ground where plants, crops, fences, posts or other objects were uprooted, mud wallowing holes; mass of pellets or tubular segments, usually near uprooted plants

Activity: diurnal, nocturnal, crepuscular; feeds for up to several hours, sits down to rest for up to 2 hours, then feeds again

Tracks: front hoof 2½-3" (6-7.5 cm) long, hind hoof slightly smaller, widely split at the front with a point in front; neat line of paired tracks, slightly offset; hind hooves fall near fore prints (no direct register) when walking

Stan's Notes: Spanish explorer Hernando de Soto brought pigs to Florida in 1539. Most Wild Hogs today are descendants of the European wild hogs that were introduced into the United States for food or sporting purposes. Some are the progeny of escaped domestic swine that became feral over just a couple generations. Wild and domestic hogs can and do interbreed, producing traits of both species such as a cartilaginous, flexible snout. Now found in over half of the United States, mainly in the South, with range expanding northward.

Wild Hogs prefer forests that produce acorn crops. In the absence of this, they will live in open woodlands and other areas not far from water. Their presence has a noticeable impact on native wildlife and plant life, as well as on crops and livestock, and, for this reason, the animals are not welcome in many places. Other areas, however, embrace their presence with managed hunting. By pushing out native species, they represent one of the most serious conservation threats.

Also called Feral Pig, Wild Boar, Russian Wild Boar and Razorback. A female (sow) and her young (piglets) will feed together and sometimes join other groups in herds of up to 35 individuals. The male (boar) tends to be solitary unless it is breeding season. Boars will fight, using their tusks to determine dominance and the right to breed.

Piglets stay with their mother for a year. They are usually brown with pale longitudinal body stripes at birth, and become sexually mature at just 18 months of age.

Black Bear
Ursus americanus

Family: Bears (Ursidae)

Size: L 4½-6' (1.4-1.8 m); T 3-7" (7.5-18 cm); H 3-3½' (.9-1.1 m)

Weight: M 100-900 lb. (45-405 kg); F 90-525 lb. (41-236 kg)

Description: Nearly all black, sometimes brown, tan or cinnamon. Short round ears. Light brown snout. May have a small white patch on its chest. Short tail, which often goes unnoticed.

Origin/Age: native; 15-30 years

Compare: The only bear species in Florida.

Habitat: all forest types, grasslands

Home: den, underneath a fallen tree or in a rock crevice or cave, may dig a den 5-6' (1.5-1.8 m) deep with a small cavity at the end; male sometimes hibernates on the ground without shelter

Food: omnivore; leaves, nuts, roots, fruit, berries, grass, insects, fish, small mammals, carrion

Sounds: huffs, puffs or grunts and groans when walking, loud snorts made by air forced from nostrils, loud roars when fighting and occasionally when mating, motor-like humming when content

Breeding: Jun-Jul mating; 60-90 days gestation; implantation delayed until November after mating

Young: 1-5 (usually 2) cubs every other year in January or February; born covered with fine dark fur, weighing only ½-1 lb. (.2-.5 kg)

257

claw marks | brown morph

scat

Signs: series of long narrow scars on tree trunks, usually as high as the bear can reach, made by scratching and biting, rub marks with snagged hair on the lower part of tree trunks or on large rocks, made by rubbing and scratching when shedding its winter coat; large dark cylindrical scat or piles of loose scat, usually contains berries and nuts, may contain animal hair, undigested plant stems and roots

Activity: diurnal, nocturnal; often seen feeding during the day

Tracks: hind paw 7-9" (18-23 cm) long, 5" (13 cm) wide with 5 toes, turns inward slightly, looks like a human footprint, forepaw 4" (10 cm) long, 5" (13 cm) wide with 5 toes, claw marks on all feet; fore and hind prints are parallel, hind paws fall several inches in front of fore prints; shuffles feet when walking

Stan's Notes: Once found throughout Florida except for the Keys. Now localized to certain regions of the state. Unique to North America. Has a shuffling gait and frequently appears clumsy. It is not designed for speed, but can run up to 30 mph (48 km/h) for short distances. A powerful swimmer, however, and good at climbing trees. It has color vision, but poor eyesight and relies on smell to find most of its food. Often alone except for mating in early summer or when bears gather at a large food supply such as a garbage dump. Feeds heavily throughout summer, adding layers of fat for hibernation.

In northern parts of its range it hibernates up to five months per year starting in late fall. In Florida it appears to hibernate for a much shorter time or not at all; occasionally wakes and moves around the den in winter. Heart rate drops from 70 to 10-20 beats per minute. Body temperature drops 1-12 °F (-17 to -11 °C), which isn't enough to change mental functions. Doesn't eat, drink, defecate or urinate when hibernating despite rousing. A female can lose up to 40 percent of its body weight when hibernating.

cub

A male has a large territory up to 15 square miles (39 sq. km) that often encompasses several female territories. Males fight each other for breeding rights and usually have scars from fights. Male bears mature at 3-4 years, but don't become full size until 10-12 years. They do not help to raise the young.

Females don't breed until 2-3 years of age. A female with more body fat when entering hibernation will have more cubs than others with less fat. If a female lacks enough fat, she won't give birth. Mothers average 177 pounds (80 kg)—about 250 times the size of newborns. A short gestation and tiny cubs are the result of the reproductive process during hibernation.

male

ARE

FORMER RANGE

American Bison
Bison bison

Family: Goats, Sheep and Cattle (Bovidae)

Size: L 8-12' (2.4-3.7 m); T 12-19" (30-48 cm); H 5-6' (1.5-1.8 m)

Weight: M 1,000-2,000 lb. (450-900 kg); F 800-1,000 lb. (360-450 kg)

Description: Dark brown head, lighter brown body and large humped shoulders. Bearded with a long shaggy mane over head and shoulders. Long tuft-tipped tail. Both sexes have short curved horns, which are not shed.

Origin/Age: native; 20-25 years

Compare: A massive animal, difficult to confuse with any other. No longer roams freely in Florida. Found only in established, managed areas such as state parks and private ranches.

Habitat: grasslands, open forests

Home: does not use a den or nest, even in bad weather or winter; beds in a different spot each night, rests in the open, laying on the ground

Food: herbivore; grasses and other green plants, lichens

Sounds: often quiet; male bellows during the rut, female snorts, young bawls for mother's attention

Breeding: Jul-Aug mating; 9-10 months gestation

Young: 1 calf every 1-2 years in May or June; born with reddish brown fur, stands within 30 minutes, walks within hours of its birth, joins herd at 2-3 days, acquires hump, horns and adult coloration at 2-3 months, weaned at 6-7 months

flehmening female

Signs: saucer-like depressions in dirt (wallows), 8-10' (2.4-3 m) wide, trees and shrubs with the bark rubbed off, shallow depressions in the grass are evidence of bison beds; scat is similar to that of the domestic cow, flat round patties, 12-14" (30-36 cm) wide

scat

Activity: crepuscular; often rests during the day to chew its cud

Tracks: front hoof 6-7" (15-18 cm) long, hind hoof slightly smaller, both with opposing crescents and more pointed in the front; hind hooves fall behind and slightly to the side of fore prints; crescents widen when walking in mud or running

Stan's Notes: The largest land mammal in North America and considered unique to the New World. Sometimes called Buffalo, but not related to the Old World buffalo.

Historically, the American Bison ranged throughout most of the United States and numbered in the tens of millions. It was hunted to near extinction around the 1880s, when a government policy advocated extermination. By the early 1900s fewer than 1,000 bison remained in the country.

Bison were once widespread in northern Florida, with extirpation occurring in the mid-1800s. Now all bison in Florida are a result of private herds managed on ranches and state parks.

Centuries ago, great herds of bison would migrate long distances between summer and winter grounds. Because bison are now kept behind fences in managed herds, they no longer migrate.

Gregarious, gathering in large herds of nearly 100 bison, mainly females (cows) and calves. Can be seen rolling and rubbing in wallows to relieve insect bites. Males (bulls) are usually on their own or in a small group in fall and winter. A dominant bull will join a maternal herd late in summer before the rut. Cows mature at 2-3 years and stay fertile for about 24 hours. A bull will curl its upper lip and extend its neck (flehmening) when around cows, perhaps to detect estrus. Bulls "tend" cows that are entering estrus rather than maintaining harems. Competing bulls strut near each other, showing off their large profile. Mature bulls sometimes face each other, charge, crash headfirst and use their massive necks to push each other. Fights rarely result in injury. Sometimes hooking or goring occurs.

sparring

Spinner Dolphin
Stenella longirostris

Family: Marine Dolphins (Delphinidae)

Size: L 5-7' (1.5-2.1 m)

Weight: 100-175 lb. (45-179 kg)

Description: Very small dolphin with a dark upper body and white-to-pink belly. Dark stripe on sides. Long narrow snout (beak). Small round eyes on sides of head just behind the line of the jaw. Breathing hole on top of head behind the eyes. Large fin on the back (dorsal) curves back and points toward the tail (falcate). Short, thick and powerful tail. Long flippers.

Origin/Age: native to waters far off the coast of Florida, the Outer Continental Shelf and the entire Atlantic Ocean, Gulf of Mexico and beyond; 20-25 years

Compare: Spinner Dolphin is much smaller than Bottlenose Dolphin (pg. 273), which has a shorter snout and does not spin when leaping from the water.

Habitat: open seas

Home: roams open waters with no well-defined territory, often following seasonal patterns; rests in open water near coral reefs

Food: ichthyophagous; fish, squid, invertebrates

Sounds: series of squeaks, whistles, chirps, growls, barks and chuckles above and below water

Breeding: Jun-Aug mating; 10-11 months gestation

Young: 1 calf every 2-3 years; born swimming, nurses for up to 2 years

spinning

Signs: shadows of large individuals swimming in groups of up to 50 individuals, riding bow waves of boats, feeding around fishing and shrimp boats, individuals breaking the surface of the water, leaping into the air, spinning on the long axis, often re-entering the water with a large splash

Activity: diurnal, nocturnal; active year-round

Tracks: none

Stan's Notes: This is a very small dolphin not seen near the shore. Mainly found beyond the Outer Continental Shelf. Very agile and fast, with a smooth, streamlined, compact body. Common name "Spinner" was given for the way it leaps out of the water into the air, spinning. Often sprints to leap from the water, spinning on its long axis several times before splashing back into the water. Often in very large groups called pods. Seen riding the bow waves of large ships.

Feeds mostly on fish and squid. Adults have 42-62 teeth in each jaw. Requires less sleep than most mammal species. Rests during the day and night. Sleeps by resting and floating near the surface. Still needs to surface to breathe, even while sleeping.

There have been more than 25 species of dolphins and whales documented in Florida. However, many of these are only known because of one or two sightings or from one individual washing up onshore dead after a major storm.

Appears to be common and widespread around the world, with stable populations. Has suffered population declines in the past as a result of the tuna fishing industry.

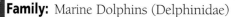

Atlantic Spotted Dolphin
Stenella frontalis

Family: Marine Dolphins (Delphinidae)

Size: L 6-6½' (1.8-2 m)

Weight: 250-275 lb. (113-124 kg)

Description: Smooth purplish gray body covered with white spots, especially on the sides. Nearly white belly. Often appears black from a distance. Short stocky snout (beak). Small round eyes on sides of head just behind the line of the jaw. Breathing hole on top of head behind eyes. Large fin on the back (dorsal) curves back and points toward the tail (falcate). Short, thick powerful tail. Long flippers. Some individuals have more spots than others. Male is longer and heavier than the female.

Origin/Age: native to waters off the coast of Florida and the entire Atlantic Ocean; 20-25 years

Compare: Smaller than the Bottlenose Dolphin (pg. 273), which has shorter flippers and lacks white spots.

Habitat: open seas, deeper bays, inlets

Home: roams open waters with no well-defined territory, often following seasonal patterns; rests in open water near coral reefs

Food: ichthyophagous; fish, squid, invertebrates

Sounds: series of squeaks, whistles, chirps, growls, barks and chuckles above and below water

Breeding: Jun-Aug mating; 12 months gestation

Young: 1 calf every 2-3 years; born swimming, nurses for up to 1 year

Signs: shadows of large individuals swimming in groups of up to 50 individuals, riding bow waves of boats, feeding around fishing and shrimp boats, individuals breaking the surface of the water, leaping into the air or surfacing for air just offshore

Activity: diurnal, nocturnal; active year-round

Tracks: none

Stan's Notes: A small dolphin, often appearing very dark from a distance. Shows a large number of small white spots when seen up close. A congregation of spots results in a blaze or white stripe on the side. Amount of spots is highly variable among individuals.

Less common than the Bottlenose Dolphin (pg. 273). Doesn't do well in captivity and is not as familiar to the general public as the Bottlenose. Often in groups, known as pods or schools, of 10-20 dolphins; sometimes in larger groups of up to 50 individuals.

Occurring only in warm waters of the Atlantic, it is the second most common dolphin in the Gulf of Mexico. More common offshore than near shore, usually never closer than 5 miles (8 km) out. When near shore, it is thought to be responding to prey items heading toward shallow waters.

Has a smooth, streamlined body. Adults have 60-84 teeth. Young are born in spring and summer and lack spots. All ride the bow waves of large ships and jump out of the water.

The Delphinidae family has 33 species of dolphins and spouted whales, which are closely related. Dolphins and porpoises are very similar, but different. Both are air-breathing marine mammals, but the porpoise has a round head and lacks the beak (snout) of the dolphin. The dorsal fin on the back of the porpoise is small and triangular compared with the larger, swept-back dorsal fin of the dolphin. Because dolphins and porpoises are similar, their names are sometimes used interchangeably.

Bottlenose Dolphin
Tursiops truncatus

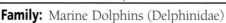

Family: Marine Dolphins (Delphinidae)

Size: L 8-8½' (2.4-2.6 m)

Weight: 450-550 lb. (203-248 kg)

Description: Smooth and streamlined gray body with a large head, short stocky snout (beak) and lighter belly. Small round eyes on the sides of head. Breathing hole on top of head behind the eyes. Large fin on the back (dorsal) curves back and points toward the tail (falcate). Short, thick powerful tail. Some individuals are darker than others. May have lighter areas of scarring from old injuries. Male is longer and heavier than the female.

Origin/Age: native to waters off the Florida coast and the Atlantic and Pacific Oceans; 20-25 years

Compare: Atlantic Spotted Dolphin (pg. 269) is smaller, stockier and has white spots on its sides. Spinner Dolphin (pg. 265) is much smaller, has a longer snout and spins when it leaps out of the water.

Habitat: open seas, bays, inlets, saltwater lagoons

Home: some stay in 1 bay, others roam open waters with no well-defined territory, often following seasonal patterns; rests in open water near coral reefs

Food: ichthyophagous; fish, squid, invertebrates

Sounds: series of squeaks, pops and chuckles above and below water

Breeding: Jun-Aug mating; 12 months gestation

Young: 1 calf every 2-3 years; born swimming, nurses for up to 1 year

breaching pod

Signs: shadows of large individuals swimming in groups, riding bow waves of boats, feeding around fishing and shrimp boats, individuals breaking the surface of the water, leaping into the air (breaching) or surfacing for air just offshore

Activity: diurnal, nocturnal; active year-round

Tracks: none

Stan's Notes: A familiar marine mammal made famous by the television show, "Flipper." Now seen in many marine or aquarium displays and museums. The Bottlenose is the most widespread and common of coastal dolphins and can be seen in relatively shallow water in lagoons, bays and inlets. The majority, however, are found well out to sea. Found throughout the temperate and tropical waters of the world.

Often in groups, called pods or schools, of 2-20 individuals, but can be seen in larger groups of up to 100 dolphins. Some groups are sedentary, remaining in a small territory of one bay; others are migratory. Populations tend to increase off the coast of Florida during fall and winter.

It is thought there are two distinct Bottlenose Dolphin forms in the Gulf of Mexico: inshore dolphins that inhabit shallow water and offshore populations remaining in deeper waters. Differences in body shape and fin size show that the inshore dolphins are adapting to shallower water.

Dolphins eat a wide variety of food depending on the abundance at the time. They eat mainly fish, including shark, tarpon, pike, rays, mullet, catfish and anchovies, along with eels. A dolphin can eat 40-50 pounds (18-23 kg) of food daily. Individuals of a group often work together when feeding. Sometimes several dolphins will herd fish into tight schools while others wait at the bottom and swim up to feed. Other times dolphins may simply chase fish into shallow water or onto beaches, where they lunge for their prey.

West Indian Manatee
Trichechus manatus

Family: Sea Cows (Trichechidae)

Size: L 10-15' (3-4.6 m)

Weight: 1,500-3,500 lb. (675-1,575 kg)

Description: An extremely large aquatic mammal. Uniformly gray overall with 2 front flippers and a large, wide round tail. Large blunt snout and tiny dark eyes. Large, flexible, prehensile upper lip, acting much like an elephant's trunk. Female is usually longer and heavier than the male.

Origin/Age: native; 50-70 years

Compare: No other extremely large mammal is found in the freshwater rivers of Florida. Hard to confuse with any other mammal. Lacks the dorsal fin of the dolphins (pp. 265-273).

Habitat: freshwater rivers, around power plants discharging warm water, not ever far from the coast

Home: freshwater rivers (moves around seasonally), estuaries, coastal water

Food: herbivore; 60 species of aquatic plants, turtle grass, mangrove leaves, algae; also eats snails and other aquatic invertebrates that attach to plants; some individuals eat small amounts of small fish

Sounds: usually silent; can grunt and groan, exhales air audibly when surfacing

Breeding: any time of year; 12 months gestation

Young: 1 calf every 2-3 years; born swimming, with a weight of about 60 pounds (27 kg); nurses for up to 1 year; stays with the mother for up to 2 years

mother and calf

Signs: shadows of large individuals swimming in freshwater rivers, estuaries and coastal waters

Activity: diurnal, nocturnal; active year-round

Tracks: none

Stan's Notes: The origin of mermaid folklore. Also known as Sea Cow, Florida Manatee or Caribbean Manatee. Slow-moving, fully aquatic, placid animal that eats plants in shallow waters. Surfaces every 3-5 minutes for air; can stay underwater up to 15 minutes. Often travels alone or in small groups. Has been in Florida for about 45 million years, according to fossil records.

Attracts tourists to Florida in winter, boosting the local economy. Congregates in the warm springs of the Crystal, Homosassa and Chassahowitzka Rivers in winter, or at power plants that release warm water. Can't survive water below 60 °F (16 °C). Disperses along the coast in summer, returning to Florida rivers for the winter. Can survive in salt water, but needs fresh water to feed. Seen as far north as Cape Cod and New York City.

There are about 3,000 manatees in the United States. Considered an endangered species by the U.S. Fish and Wildlife Service. Adult numbers are decreasing and many predict that this species could become extinct in the not-so-distant future if population trends do not change. Because the manatee moves so slowly, its number one killer is speeding motorboats. Some individuals have up to 50 distinct scars from nearly fatal boat contacts.

A very long-lived animal and slow to reproduce. Females are known as cows, males are called bulls and young are calves. Like all mammals, manatee calves obtain nutrition from their mother's milk. Calves stay at their mother's side for the first few months and range farther away as they grow up.

The manatee has special nostrils with valves to keep out water. It lacks external ears, but hears well with internal ears. Mothers and calves make soft sounds to communicate with each other.

The manatee's upper lip is prehensile, dexterous, distantly related to an elephant's trunk and acts like a vacuum cleaner. Manatees use this lip to remove algae from the backs of other manatees.

GLOSSARY

Browse: Twigs, buds and leaves that deer and other animals eat.

Canid: A member of the Wolves, Foxes and Coyote family, which includes dogs.

Carnivore: An animal, such as a mink, fox or wolf, that eats the flesh of other animals for its main nutrition.

Carrion: Dead or decaying flesh. Carrion is a significant food source for many animal species.

Cecum: The large pouch that forms the beginning of the large intestine. Also known as the blind gut.

Cheek ruff: A gathering of long stiff hairs on each side of the face of an animal, ending in a downward point. Seen in bobcats.

Coprophagy: The act of reingesting fecal pellets. Coprophagy enables rabbits and hares to gain more nourishment since the pellets pass through the digestive system a second time.

Crepuscular: Active during the early morning and late evening hours as opposed to day or night. See *diurnal* and *nocturnal*.

Cud: Food regurgitated from the first stomach to the mouth, and chewed again. Cud is produced by hoofed animals such as deer or bison, which have a four-chambered stomach (ruminants).

Dewclaw: A nonfunctional (vestigial) digit on the feet of some animals, which does not touch the ground. Seen in deer.

Direct register: The act of a hind paw landing or registering in the track left by a forepaw, resulting in two prints that appear like one track. Usually occurs when walking.

Diurnal: Active during daylight hours as opposed to nighttime hours. Opposite of *nocturnal*.

Drey: The nest of a squirrel.

Duff: The layer of decaying leaves, grasses, twigs or branches, often several inches thick, on a forest floor or prairie.

Echolocation: A sensory system in bats, dolphins and some shrews, in which inaudible, high-pitched sounds are emitted and the returning echoes are interpreted to determine the direction and distance of objects such as prey.

Estrus: A state of sexual readiness in most female animals that immediately precedes ovulation, and the time when females are most receptive to mating. Also known as heat.

Extirpate: To hunt or trap into extinction in a region or state.

Flehmen: The lift of the upper lip and grimace an animal makes when it draws air into its mouth and over its Jacobson's organ, which is thought to help analyze the scents (pheromones) wafting in the air. Frequently seen in cats, deer and bison.

Fossorial: Well suited for burrowing or digging. Describes an animal such as a mole.

Gestation: Pregnancy. The period of development in the uterus of a mammal from conception up to birth.

Grizzled: Streaked or tipped with gray, or partly gray. Describes the appearance of some fur.

Guard hairs: The long outer hairs of an animal's coat, which provide warmth. Guard hairs are typically hollow and usually thicker and darker than the soft hairs underneath.

Haul out: A well-worn trail or area on the shore where an animal, such as an otter, climbs or hauls itself out of the water.

Herbivore: An animal, such as a rabbit or deer, that eats plants for its main nutrition.

Hibernation: A torpid or lethargic state characterized by decreased heart rate, respiration and body temperature, and occurring in close quarters for long periods during winter. See *torpor*.

Hoary: Partly white or silver streaked, or tipped with white or silver. Describes the appearance of some fur.

Hummock: A low mound or ridge of earth or plants.

Insectivore: An animal, such as a shrew, that eats insects as its main nutrition.

Keratin: A hard protein that is the chief component of the hair, nails, horns and hooves of an animal.

Microflora: Bacterial life living in the gut or first stomach of an animal. Microflora help break down food and aid in the digestive process.

Midden: A mound or deposit of pine cone parts and other refuse. A midden is evidence of a favorite feeding site of an animal such as a squirrel.

Morph: One of various distinct shapes, structural differences or colors of an animal. Color morphs do not change during the life of an animal.

Nictitating membrane: A second, inner eyelid, usually translucent, that protects and moistens the eye.

Nocturnal: Active during nighttime hours as opposed to daylight hours. Opposite of *diurnal*.

Nonretractile: That which cannot be drawn back or in. Describes the claws of a dog. Opposite of *retractile*.

Omnivore: An animal, such as a bear, that eats a wide range of foods including plants, insects and the flesh of other animals as its main nutrition.

Patagium: A thin membrane extending from the body to the front and hind limbs, forming a wing-like extension. Seen in flying squirrels and bats.

Population: All individuals of a species within a specific area.

Predator: An animal that hunts, kills and eats other animals. See *prey*.

Prey: An animal that is hunted, killed and eaten by a predator. See *predator*.

Retractile: That which can be drawn back or in. Describes the claws of a cat. Opposite of *nonretractile*.

Rut: An annually recurring condition of sexual readiness and reproductive activity in mammals, such as deer, that usually occurs in autumn. See *estrus*.

Scat: The fecal droppings of an animal.

Scent marking: A means of marking territory, signaling sexual availability or communicating an individual's identity. An animal scent marks with urine, feces or by secreting a tiny amount of odorous liquid from a gland, usually near the base of the tail, chin or feet, onto specific areas such as rocks, trees and stumps.

Semiprehensile: Suited for partially seizing, grasping or holding, especially by wrapping around an object, but not a means of full support. Describes the tail of an opossum.

Stride: In larger animals, the distance between individual tracks. In smaller animals, such as weasels, the distance between sets of tracks.

Subterranean: Below the surface of the earth.

Tannin: A bitter-tasting astringent found in the nuts of many plant species.

Torpor: A torpid or lethargic state resembling hibernation, characterized by decreased heart rate, respiration and body temperature, but usually shorter, lasting from a few hours to several days or weeks. See *hibernation*.

Tragus: A fleshy projection in the central part of the ear of most bats. The size and shape of the tragus may be used to help identify some bat species.

Tree rub: An area on small to medium trees where the bark has been scraped or stripped off. A tree rub is made by a male deer polishing his antlers in preparation for the rut.

Velvet: A soft, furry covering on antlers that contains many blood vessels, which support antler growth. Velvet is shed when antlers reach full size. Seen in the Deer family.

Vibrissae: Sensitive bristles and hairs, such as whiskers, that help an animal feel its way in the dark. Vibrissae are often on the face, legs and tail.

Wallow: A depression in the ground that is devoid of vegetation, where an animal, such as a bison, rolls around on its back to "bathe" in dirt.

HELPFUL RESOURCES

Emergency

For an animal bite, please seek medical attention at an emergency room or call 911. Injured or orphaned animals should be turned over to a licensed wildlife rehabilitator. Check your local listings for a rehabilitator near you.

Web Pages

The internet is a valuable place to learn more about mammals. You may find studying mammals on the net a fun way to discover additional information about them or to spend a long winter night. These web sites will assist you in your pursuit of mammals. If a web address doesn't work (they often change a bit), just enter the name of the group into a search engine to track down the new web address.

Site and Address:

Smithsonian Institution - North American Mammals
www.mnh.si.edu/mna

The American Society of Mammalogists
www.mammalsociety.org

National Wildlife Rehabilitators Association
www.nwrawildlife.org/home.asp

International Wildlife Rehabilitation Council
www.iwrc-online.org

Florida Fish and Wildlife Conservation Commission
http://myfwc.com

Author Stan Tekiela's home page
www.naturesmart.com

Florida's Artiodactyla Order

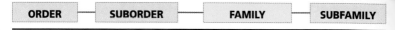

| ORDER | SUBORDER | FAMILY | SUBFAMILY |

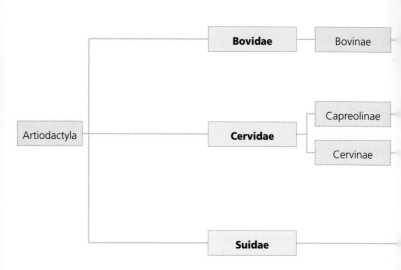

Artiodactyla

Bovidae — Bovinae

Cervidae — Capreolinae

Cervinae

Suidae

American Bison pg. 261
Bison bison

Key Deer pg. 241
Odocoileus virginianus clavium
White-tailed Deer pg. 245
Odocoileus virginianus

Sambar Deer pg. 249
Cervus unicolor

Wild Hog pg. 253
Sus scrofa

Box colors match the
corresponding section of the book.

Florida's Carnivora Order

| ORDER | SUBORDER | FAMILY | SUBFAMILY |

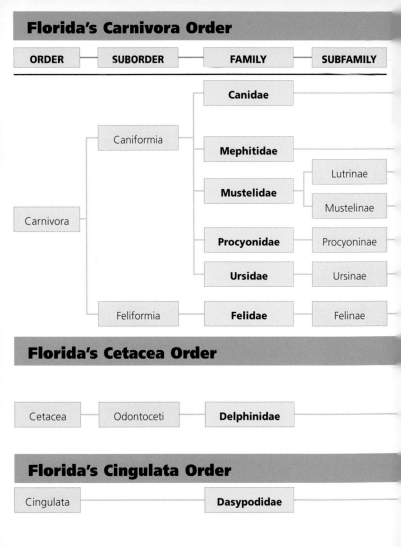

Carnivora	Caniformia	**Canidae**	
		Mephitidae	
		Mustelidae	Lutrinae
			Mustelinae
		Procyonidae	Procyoninae
		Ursidae	Ursinae
	Feliformia	**Felidae**	Felinae

Florida's Cetacea Order

| Cetacea | Odontoceti | **Delphinidae** | |

Florida's Cingulata Order

| Cingulata | | **Dasypodidae** | |

Meat-eating Predators

Gray Fox pg. 213
Urocyon cinereoargenteus

Red Fox pg. 217
Vulpes vulpes

Coyote pg. 221
Canis latrans
Red Wolf pg. 225
Canis rufus

Eastern Spotted Skunk pg. 189
Spilogale putorius

Northern River Otter pg. 185
Lontra canadensis

Striped Skunk pg. 193
Mephitis mephitis

Long-tailed Weasel pg. 177
Mustela frenata
Mink pg. 181
Mustela vison

Northern Raccoon pg. 197
Procyon lotor

White-nosed Coati pg. 201
Nasua narica

Black Bear pg. 257
Ursus americanus

Jaguarundi pg. 229
Herpailurus yagouaroundi

Bobcat pg. 233
Lynx rufus

Florida Panther pg. 237
Puma concolor conyi

Dolphins

Spinner Dolphin pg. 265
Stenella longirostris
Atlantic Spotted Dolphin pg. 269
Stenella frontalis

Bottlenose Dolphin pg. 273
Tursiops truncatus

Armadillo

Nine-banded Armadillo pg. 205
Dasypus novemcinctus

Box colors match the
corresponding section of the book.

Florida's Chiroptera Order

ORDER	SUBORDER	FAMILY	SUBFAMILY

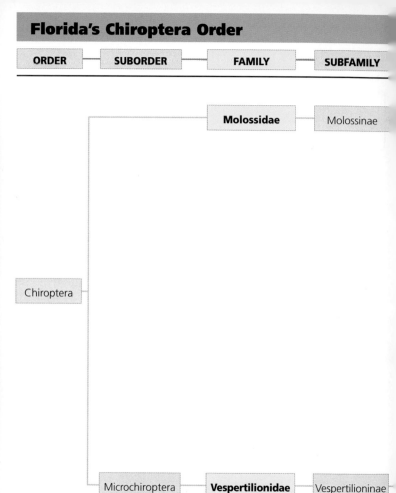

Molossidae — Molossinae

Chiroptera

Microchiroptera — **Vespertilionidae** — Vespertilioninae

Brazilian Free-tailed Bat pg. 127
Tadarida brasiliensis

Little Mastiff Bat pg. 131
Molossus molossus

Wagner's Bonneted Bat pg. 131
Eumops glaucinus

Little Brown Bat pg. 130
Myotis lucifugus
Northern Myotis pg. 130
Myotis septentrionalis
Indiana Bat pg. 131
Myotis sodalis
Gray Myotis pg. 131
Myotis grisescens
Southeastern Bat pg. 131
Myotis austroriparius

Eastern Pipistrelle pg. 130
Pipistrellus subflavus

Evening Bat pg. 130
Nycticeius humeralis

Big Brown Bat pg. 130
Eptesicus fuscus

Silver-haired Bat pg. 130
Lasionycteris noctivagans

Eastern Red Bat pg. 131
Lasiurus borealis
Hoary Bat pg. 131
Lasiurus cinereus
Northern Yellow Bat pg. 131
Lasiurus intermedius
Seminole Bat pg. 131
Lasiurus seminolus

Rafinesque's Big-eared Bat pg. 131
Corynorhinus rafinesquii

Box colors match the
corresponding section of the book.

Florida's Didelphimorphia Order

ORDER	SUBORDER	FAMILY	SUBFAMILY
Didelphimorphia		**Didelphidae**	Didelphinae

Florida's Insectivora Order

		Soricidae	Soricinae
Insectivora		**Talpidae**	Talpinae

Florida's Lagomorpha Order

Lagomorpha	**Leporidae**	

Florida's Primates Order

Primates	Haplorrhini	**Cebidae**	Saimirinae
		Cercopithecidae	Cercopithecinae

Marsupial

Virginia Opossum pg. 209
Didelphis virginiana

Shrews and Moles

Least Shrew pg. 35
Cryptotis parva

Southeastern Shrew pg. 39
Sorex longirostris

Southern Short-tailed Shrew pg. 43
Blarina carolinensis

Star-nosed Mole pg. 47
Condylura cristata

Eastern Mole pg. 51
Scalopus aquaticus

Rabbits and Hare

Marsh Rabbit pg. 165
Sylvilagus palustris

Eastern Cottontail pg. 169
Sylvilagus floridanus

Black-tailed Jackrabbit pg. 173
Lepus californicus

Monkeys

Squirrel Monkey pg. 157
Saimiri sciureus

Rhesus Monkey pg. 161
Macaca mulatta

Box colors match the
corresponding section of the book.

Florida's Rodentia Order

| ORDER | — | SUBORDER | — | FAMILY | — | SUBFAMILY |

Rodentia	Castorimorpha	**Castoridae**	
		Geomyidae	
	Hystricomorpha	**Cavidae**	Hydrochoerinae
		Myocastoridae	
	Myomorpha	**Muridae**	Arvicolinae
			Murinae
			Sigmodontinae
	Sciuromorpha	**Sciuridae**	Sciurinae
			Xerinae

Florida's Sirenia Order

| Sirenia | | **Trichechidae** | Trichechinae |

Rodents

American Beaver pg. 119
Castor canadensis

Southeastern Pocket Gopher pg. 153
Geomys pinetis

Capybara pg. 123
Hydrochoerus hydrochaeris

Nutria pg. 115
Myocastor coypus

Golden Mouse pg. 67
Ochrotomys nuttalli

Pine Vole pg. 103
Microtus pinetorum
Salt Marsh Vole pg. 107
Microtus pennsylvanicus

Eastern Harvest Mouse pg. 55
Reithrodontomys humulis

Round-tailed Muskrat pg. 111
Neofiber alleni

Oldfield Mouse pg. 59
Peromyscus polionotus
Cotton Mouse pg. 71
Peromyscus gossypinus

House Mouse pg. 63
Mus musculus

Florida Mouse pg. 75
Podomys floridanus

Black Rat pg. 87
Rattus rattus
Norway Rat pg. 95
Rattus norvegicus

Key Rice Rat pg. 79
Oryzomys argentatus
Marsh Rice Rat pg. 83
Oryzomys palustris

Southern Flying Squirrel pg. 137
Glaucomys volans

Hispid Cotton Rat pg. 91
Sigmodon hispidus

Eastern Gray Squirrel pg. 141
Sciurus carolinensis
Red-bellied Squirrel pg. 145
Sciurus aureogaster
Fox Squirrel pg. 149
Sciurus niger shermanii

Eastern Woodrat pg. 99
Neotoma floridana

Eastern Chipmunk pg. 133
Tamias striatus

Manatee

West Indian Manatee pg. 277
Trichechus manatus

Box colors match the
corresponding section of the book.

295

CHECK LIST/INDEX

Use the boxes to check the mammals you've seen.

☐ Armadillo, Nine-banded 205
☐ Bat, Big Brown 130
☐ Bat, Brazilian Free-tailed 127
☐ Bat, Eastern Red 131
☐ Bat, Evening 130
☐ Bat, Hoary 131
☐ Bat, Indiana 131
☐ Bat, Little Brown 130
☐ Bat, Little Mastiff 131
☐ Bat, Northern Yellow 131
☐ Bat, Rafinesque's Big-eared 131
☐ Bat, Seminole 131
☐ Bat, Silver-haired 130
☐ Bat, Southeastern 131
☐ Bat, Wagner's Bonneted 131
☐ Bear, Black 257
☐ Beaver, American 119
☐ Bison, American 261
☐ Bobcat 233
☐ Capybara 123
☐ Chipmunk, Eastern 133
☐ Coati, White-nosed 201
☐ Cottontail, Eastern 169
☐ Coyote 221
☐ Deer, Key 241

▣ Deer, Sambar 249
▣ Deer, White-tailed 245
▣ Dolphin, Atlantic Spotted 269
▣ Dolphin, Bottlenose 273
▣ Dolphin, Spinner 265
▣ Fox, Gray 213
▣ Fox, Red 217
▣ Gopher, Southeastern Pocket 153
▣ Hog, Wild 253
▣ Jackrabbit, Black-tailed 173
▣ Jaguarundi 229
▣ Manatee, West Indian 277
▣ Mink 181
▣ Mole, Eastern 51
▣ Mole, Star-nosed 47
▣ Monkey, Rhesus 161
▣ Monkey, Squirrel 157
▣ Mouse, Cotton 71
▣ Mouse, Eastern Harvest 55
▣ Mouse, Florida 75
▣ Mouse, Golden 67
▣ Mouse, House 63
▣ Mouse, Oldfield 59
▣ Muskrat, Round-tailed 111
▣ Myotis, Gray 131
▣ Myotis, Northern 130
▣ Nutria 115

297

☐ Opossum, Virginia. 209
☐ Otter, Northern River. 185
☐ Panther, Florida 237
☐ Pipistrelle, Eastern 130
☐ Rabbit, Marsh 165
☐ Raccoon, Northern 197
☐ Rat, Black 87
☐ Rat, Hispid Cotton. 91
☐ Rat, Key Rice 79
☐ Rat, Marsh Rice 83
☐ Rat, Norway 95
☐ Shrew, Least 35
☐ Shrew, Southeastern 39
☐ Shrew, Southern Short-tailed. 43
☐ Skunk, Eastern Spotted 189
☐ Skunk, Striped. 193
☐ Squirrel, Eastern Gray 141
☐ Squirrel, Fox 149
☐ Squirrel, Red-bellied 145
☐ Squirrel, Southern Flying 137
☐ Vole, Pine 103
☐ Vole, Salt Marsh 107
☐ Weasel, Long-tailed. 177
☐ Wolf, Red 225
☐ Woodrat, Eastern 99

PHOTO CREDITS

All photos are copyright of their respective photographers. To the best of the publisher's knowledge, all photos were of live mammals. Some were photographed in a controlled condition.

Dr. J. Scott Altenbach: 131 (Little Mastiff, Northern Yellow, Seminole)

Chuck Babbitt: 264

Roger W. Barbour: 58, 131 (Gray, Wagner's)

John Bokma: 146

Rick and Nora Bowers: 84, 90, 92, 126, 128 (main), 202 (top and middle insets), 228, 230

Mary Clay/Dembinsky Photo Associates: 190 (main)

E. R. Degginger/Dembinsky Photo Associates: 36, 48

Larry Ditto/KAC Productions: 354 (main)

Richard B. Forbes, Ph.D.: 116

Jeff Gore/Florida Fish and Wildlife Conservation Commission: 60

Monica Harris/U.S. Fish and Wildlife Service: 250

Gary Kramer: 254 (middle inset)

Greg Lasley Nature Photography: 144

Tom & Pat Leeson: 236, 238

Stephen LeQuier: 160, 162

Barry Mansell: 68, 74, 76 (both), 110, 112, 152, 154 (all)

Maslowski Productions: 34, 46, 138 (main), 150 (Big Cypress), 176, 179, 252, 254 (top and bottom insets)

Gary Meszaros/Dembinsky Photo Associates: 108 (main), 109

Jeff Mondragon: 268, 270, 272

Skip Moody/Dembinsky Photo Associates: 49

Philip Myers: 102

PHOTO CREDITS *(continued)*

Jake Osborne: 248

Stan Osolinski/Dembinsky Photo Associates: 178

Michael Palmer: 114

Ed Pivorun: 38, 40

Chris Scott: 78, 80

Ann and Rob Simpson: 42, 72 (inset), 100

Stan Tekiela: 50, 52 (all), 62, 64 (both), 65, 82, 86, 88, 94, 96 (both), 106, 108 (inset), 118, 120 (all), 122, 124, 128 (inset), 130 (Little Brown, Northern, Big Brown, Silver-haired), 131 (Eastern Red, Hoary), 132, 134 (all), 136, 138 (both insets), 139, 140, 142 (all), 143, 148, 150 (main, Eastern, black morph), 151, 164, 166, 168, 170 (all), 171, 172, 174 (both), 180, 182 (all), 183, 184, 186 (all), 188, 190 (inset), 191, 192, 194 (all), 195, 196, 198 (both), 199, 200, 202 (main, bottom inset), 204, 206 (all), 208, 210 (all), 211, 212, 214 (all), 215 (both), 216, 218 (all), 220, 222 (all), 223, 224, 226 (both insets), 232, 234 (all), 235, 238 (both insets), 239, 240, 242 (both), 244, 246 (all), 247, 256, 258 (all), 259, 260, 262 (all), 263, 274 (both)

Merlin D. Tuttle/Bat Conservation International, Inc.: 130 (Pipistrelle, Evening), 131 (Indiana, Southeastern, Rafinesque's)

John and Gloria Tveten: 37 (bottom inset), 98, 104

John and Gloria Tveten/KAC Productions: 44, 54, 56, 66, 70, 72 (main)

R. Wayne VanDevender: 37 (top inset)

Dale Walsh: 266

www.cameraview.com: 226 (main)

www.FloridaNaturePhotography.com: 150 (white morph)

www.oceangrant.com: 276, 278

www.richturkphotos.com: 156, 158

ABOUT THE AUTHOR

Naturalist, wildlife photographer and writer Stan Tekiela is the originator of the popular state-specific field guides such as *Birds of Florida Field Guide*. For over two decades, Stan has authored more than 100 field guides, nature appreciation books and wildlife audio CDs covering nearly every state in the nation, presenting many species of birds, mammals, reptiles and amphibians, trees, wildflowers and cacti. Holding a Bachelor of Science degree in Natural History from the University of Minnesota and as an active professional naturalist for more than 20 years, Stan studies and photographs wildlife throughout the United States and has received various national and regional awards for his books and photographs. Also a well-known columnist and radio personality, his syndicated column appears in over 20 newspapers and his wildlife programs are broadcast on a number of Midwest radio stations. He is a member of the North American Nature Photography Association and Canon Professional Services. Stan resides in Victoria, Minnesota, with his wife, Katherine, and daughter, Abigail. He can be contacted via his web page at www.naturesmart.com.

Identifying Florida's mammals is now easy and enjoyable!

Make mammal identification simpler, more informative and productive

- all 77 of Florida's mammals, from mice to manatees
- facts about size, habitat, range, young and more
- times each animal is most likely to be active and signs that it might leave such as rubs and scrapes
- track patterns, size details and scat photos
- Stan's naturalist notes and gee-whiz facts

About the Author

Stan Tekiela is a naturalist, wildlife photographer and the originator of many popular state-specific field guides. He has authored over 100 field guides, nature books and audio CDs, presenting many species of birds, mammals, reptiles and amphibians, trees, wildflowers and cacti.

COLLECT ALL FIVE FLORIDA FIELD GUIDES

$14.95

Adventure Publications, Inc.
820 Cleveland St. S
Cambridge, MN 55008
1-800-678-7006
www.adventurepublications.net
ISBN-13: 978-1-59193-251-2
ISBN-10: 1-59193-251-3

ISBN 1-59193-251-3

9 781591 932512